LIVING BELIEF

For Gerhard Sauter

LIVING BELIEF

Being Christian, Being Human

John Barton

continuum

Published by Continuum

The Tower Building, 11 York Road, London SE1 7NX
15 East 26th Street, Suite 1703, New York, NY 10010

www.continuumbooks.com

British Library Cataloguing-in-Publication Data
A catalogue record for this book is available from the British Library

ISBN 082648851X (paperback)

Typeset by Free Range Book Design & Production
Printed on acid-free paper in Great Britain by MPG Books Ltd, Cornwall

Contents

Introduction

Down the centuries Christians have spent much effort in defining their beliefs. One result is the various creeds that sum up what you must believe to be counted a Christian. Yet, strangely enough, the beliefs to which the creeds bear witness are not always the beliefs by which Christians actually live from day to day. Few spend much time, for example, reflecting on the doctrine of the Trinity, on the union of divine and human in Jesus Christ, or in theories about the Holy Spirit in the life of the Church – even though these are central to what is in the creeds.

On the other hand, there are many beliefs that animate much Christian life but are not found in the creeds at all. For many Christians, the heart of their faith is to do with making sense of the world, relating to the Christ known in prayer and action, living constructively with others, fostering certain kinds of attitude and relationships. The theologian will be able to relate this to the doctrines of the creeds, but most Christians are not concerned with such lines of connection, which often seem rather theoretical.

In this book we shall look at some areas of what I call 'living belief'. I have chosen four such areas, and each has two chapters devoted to it. The first is the idea of suffering with Christ, which has considerable resonance for some, especially perhaps for those in a Catholic tradition of faith. It is central to some people's understanding of their own, and other's, sufferings, and it raises questions about how we can be close to God in times of difficulty and distress.

The second idea is that of a divine plan for human life, and particularly for our own life. For many Christians – perhaps especially those in a Protestant tradition – trying to discern what God wants them to do day by day and minute by minute forms the heart of their spiritual journey. It becomes a way of 'making sense' of life.

Thirdly, Christians of all persuasions believe that their faith must not be turned in on itself, but must open out in care for others. Nowadays this is often expressed in terms of all Christians having a 'ministry' to others. Whatever they think about the official ministry of whichever church they belong to, many see themselves as committed to ministering to others by the way they live life in the world. In traditional Protestantism this has been expressed in terms of the 'priesthood of all believers'; in Catholicism, increasingly since the Second Vatican Council, it has meant that laypeople see themselves as having a ministry alongside that of the clergy, which means that they need to develop pastoral skills of their own.

There are many Christian 'virtues' to which Christians aspire: love, peace, faith, hope, and so on. But I have chosen to include two chapters on joy, which gives encouragement to all on a spiritual path and helps them to persevere in Christian discipleship.

INTRODUCTION

Other themes could equally well have been chosen, and there is no suggestion that these four in any way cover the whole ground of 'living belief'. But I hope they will strike a chord with readers looking for ways of reflecting on the practice of a Christian lifestyle. The subtitle expresses the conviction that being a Christian is a way of being human, and presupposes a common humanity shared also with those who are not believers. Evangelism is sterile if it ever forgets this.

The book originated in two days of Lent Lectures given to clergy in the Winchester Diocese in 1994, when I was the Canon Theologian at the Cathedral. The material has been revised and reshaped, partly in response to reactions from those who heard the lectures. I am grateful to the then bishop, Colin James, for inviting me to speak. I used and reworked some of the material for an ordination retreat delivered in the Bristol Diocese in 1999, and other ideas have been tried out on various congregations to whom I have preached. Thanks are also due to Philip Law, my commissioning editor, who has constantly encouraged me to publish a Lent book.

In writing, I have been strongly aware of a debt to my old friend Gerhard Sauter, Emeritus Professor of Systematic Theology in the Protestant Theology Faculty in the University of Bonn, whose work makes an explicit appearance in Chapters 3 and 4. It is a great pleasure to dedicate the book to him on the occasion of his seventieth birthday. Needless to say, he is not responsible for the use I have made of ideas I learned from him.

John Barton

1. Walking in the Way of the Cross

In the Church of England's new prayer book, *Common Worship*, the following prayer is used on the third Sunday in Lent:

> Almighty God,
> whose most dear Son went not up to joy before he
>   suffered pain,
> and entered not into glory before he was crucified:
> mercifully grant that we, walking in the way of the
>   cross,
> may find it none other than the way of life and peace;
> through Jesus Christ your Son our Lord,
> who is alive and reigns with you,
> in the unity of the Holy Spirit,
> one God, now and for ever.

In the American Episcopal Church the prayer is used on the Monday in Holy Week.

The idea of following Christ on the way of the cross has never been officially declared to be part of the Christian faith – it is not really the kind of belief that could be officially 'defined'. Even books on Christian ethics do not often make it the centre of their concern. Yet it is at the heart of many people's understanding of the gospel and of the Christian life. The creeds define who Christ is, but for most Christians the idea of a discipleship in which Christ, however exactly he is understood, is followed on his *via dolorosa*, has much greater religious power than credal definitions.

The idea of imitating Christ in his passion goes back a long way in Christian thought – some would say to the very beginning. It seems to begin life as a way of thinking about martyrdom, which is in an obvious way suffering with Christ, suffering in his cause and for his sake. It is already there in 1 Peter 2.20–4 in a passage addressed to Christian slaves:

> If you endure when you are beaten for doing wrong, where is the credit in that? But if you endure when you do right and suffer for it, you have God's approval. For to this you have been called, because Christ also suffered for you, leaving you an example, so that you should follow in his steps. 'He committed no sin, and no deceit was found in his mouth'. When he was abused, he did not return abuse; when he suffered, he did not threaten; but he entrusted himself to the one who judges justly. He himself bore our sins in his body on the cross, so that, free from sins, we might live for righteousness; by his wounds you have been healed.

And perhaps it is there in Paul's mysterious words in Colossians 1.24, 'I am now rejoicing in my sufferings for

6

your sake, and in my flesh I am completing what is lacking in Christ's afflictions for the sake of his body, that is, the church.' But of course in the Gospels too we have Jesus' call, 'If any want to become my disciples, let them deny themselves and take up their cross and follow me.' And the disciples in Acts 5.41, who had been punished by the Jewish court, 'rejoiced that they were considered worthy to suffer dishonour for the sake of the name'.

At some point the idea of suffering with Christ in the sense of sharing literally in a passion and death like his, and in his cause, turned into a metaphor for any suffering a Christian might endure. This has already happened in Luke 9.23, Luke's version of the saying about taking up the cross, where disciples are to deny themselves and take up their cross *daily*. This must mean accepting privations and hardships *as if* they were the cross of Christ. Luke's Jesus looks beyond his own time, when his followers are to be challenged (just as they are in Matthew and Mark) to follow him even though it may lead to crucifixion. He foresees a time when the way of the cross will mean something less literal and more general: the sufferings of life, whatever they may be, borne with endurance for Christ's sake. That is the image of suffering with Christ that has come down to us in Christian tradition.

In the process a further theme has been added, derived from an ascetical tradition whose roots are older than Christianity. This theme is the importance of deliberately taking on sufferings, even those that do not come one's way as an inevitable part of being a disciple, and bearing them as if they were the cross. By this means anyone, however rich and safe and comfortable, can still walk the way of the cross by taking on voluntary pain and suffering. This idea has a long pedigree, especially in Catholic Christianity, though it has been found in many types of Protestantism, too. Protestants tend to be unsympathetic to voluntary pain and abstinence, and have little time for a saint such as, for example, Thérèse of Lisieux, or the Desert Fathers, or many of the Celtic saints with their regime of punitive fasting and penance. Nevertheless, there has been a deliberate austerity of lifestyle, especially in what we might call the Puritan strand of Protestantism. This has certainly seen the Christian life as a pilgrimage lived by following in the steps of Jesus Christ, and has expected hardship and pain to result from loyalty to him. Evangelical Christians are taught to expect opposition and derision from others to result from their openly professed commitment to Jesus. So 'suffering with Christ' is an idea few Christians would reject, even though they may define it in different ways.

But nowadays there is a huge problem about this way of thinking: to most modern people it can sound pathological. We can distinguish four stages:

- Enduring suffering for a good cause that anyone must admire is not problematic;
- Rejoicing in such suffering is higher than most of us can aspire to, but is also deeply admirable – you are saying that your commitment to the cause (or person, or truth) in question is greater than your commitment to your own well-being;
- Seeking out sufferings to be endured begins, to most modern minds, to seem a bit dubious; and

- Inflicting sufferings on yourself deliberately now has a psychological name all to itself (masochism), and the vast majority of modern people pity it at best, and feel sickened by it at worst.

The churches have all recognized this sliding scale, which ends in something deeply unhealthy, and religious communities with few exceptions have abolished hair shirts, scourges, and other ways of giving themselves pain, and have returned to what is recognized more or less universally as an ancient type of asceticism: vigilance in prayer, some simple fasting or moderation in eating, austerity of lifestyle, but all in the service of Christian joy and with no implied criticism of normal human pleasure. This change – which does not relate to any credal or official formulations of doctrine – represents a quite radical change in what is actually believed about the goodness of the created world and about the nature of the life of discipleship. If we are to go on using the language of 'suffering with Christ', we need to understand the shift involved.

Revulsion at talk of sharing Christ's sufferings is not just a matter of falling into line with the modern world or buying into modern psychology; it has older Christian roots. At first sight this may not seem to be so. In the Middle Ages, after all, contemplation of the wounds and the human sufferings of Christ was already pioneered by the early Franciscans, and by the time of the Reformation it was widespread in Europe. The 'man of sorrows', a life-sized representation of Christ crowned with thorns, became widespread in central Europe. The churches of the Reformation accepted this way of thinking from their

Catholic past. In England, George Herbert's poems meditate on the Passion in a way not alien to the devotional life of medieval Europe or, indeed, of the Counter-Reformation.[1] The tradition of contemplating Christ's Passion and seeking to enter imaginatively into it became so ubiquitous that it is hard to remember that it was not found in this form in the earliest Christian centuries. In the mainline continental Reformation it continued in the Lutheran tradition, with Bach's great *Passions* as its climax. In them we are drawn into the Lord's sufferings by hearing the words of the Gospels, listening attentively to reflection on them in arias and choruses, and then joining in them ourselves in the chorales.

But just for this reason Luther himself is surprising. Though he greatly encouraged such extended meditation on Christ's sufferings and death, he did not encourage the imaginative or actual sharing in Christ's pain, which he had experienced as part of Catholic asceticism when he was a friar. He warned against 'mingling' our sufferings with those of Christ, blurring the distinction between what he endured and whatever we may have to endure. The hymn 'O sacred head, sore wounded', contains these lines:

In thy most bitter passion
    My heart to share doth cry,
With thee for my salvation
    Upon the cross to die.

This is a Lutheran chorale, though translated originally from a medieval Latin hymn (*Salve caput cruentatum*, ascribed to Bernard of Clairvaux, translated by Paul Gerhardt, 1607–76), but it does not express Luther's mind when it includes the idea of sharing Christ's cross. (In fact the theme of sharing Christ's sufferings is not nearly so marked in the original as it is in Robert Bridge's English translation.)

There is a major theological point here, linked to Luther's central belief in justification by faith alone and his opposition to 'works'. The sufferings of Christ are a once-and-for-all event, and though we do not know how they bring about our salvation, we must at least be convinced as Christians that nothing else does. There is not a kind of 'pool' of suffering, like the Catholic 'treasury of merits', in which Christ contributes the greater part but to which we make our own little contributions in order to secure the world's salvation. Our contribution is precisely nothing, Christ's is everything. Thus the idea of 'sharing' in Christ's sufferings is a radically unchristian idea, on Luther's way of thinking, and belongs to our all-too-human tendency to want to bring about our own salvation. When we contemplate the sufferings of Christ, as we do in a Lutheran Passion service or a Bach *Passion*, we enter imaginatively into what Christ suffered in order to realize how great was what he endured for us, and to give him fitting thanks for it. We do not do so in order to make ourselves suffer, or to add our sufferings to his as though such a thing were either necessary or possible.

Superficially this Lutheran point can be met very easily. Those who believe that our part is to share in Christ's sufferings will say that they never supposed – indeed, no Christian ever supposed – that salvation was anything other than a free gift from God, which we receive through faith but which we do nothing to deserve or bring about. To say that we must not think we suffer with Christ, because our sufferings do not earn our salvation, is to be opposed to an idea no one ever had anyway. In order for Luther to stress the 'free gift' character of salvation, and to emphasize that we cannot earn it, it was probably quite a good debating point to say that God does not require us to suffer too. But it was no more than a debating point, because Christianity has never taught that he does.

At a deeper level, though, Luther was (I believe) profoundly right to argue as he did. Christians who are devoted to the language of 'suffering with Christ' are apt to agree that our sufferings cannot contribute much (or even anything) to our salvation *because they are so puny compared with Christ's*. This theme can be found from very early times. It is there in the story that St Peter opted to be crucified upside down because he felt he was not worthy to share his Master's crucifixion; and also in Ignatius of Antioch in the early second century, travelling to his martyrdom and imploring the churches to which he wrote on his journey not to try to get him pardoned from his death sentence, so that his martyrdom might at least approximate to the sufferings of his Lord. It continues in the thoughts of all the Christians in our own day who meditate on the Passion and reflect how little they themselves suffer, and how much better it might be if they suffered more.

This frame of mind is still to be found very actively among faithful Christians. It does not come from a feeling than God demands our suffering, but it does reflect a sense that suffering is a wholly appropriate response to his love shown through the sufferings of Christ; and perhaps a feeling that if we really could suffer as Christ did, the world would be changed. I am not talking now of a pathological desire for pain, but of a sober Christian belief that, as the hymn puts it, 'Then will they know, they that love him, how all their pain is good' (another Robert Bridges translation!). It is never as much as we deserve, and *that* is why it is not enough to save us, people feel. We need Christ's sufferings, which are so much more immense than any of ours that they alone can produce human salvation. But our sufferings are blessed by God none the less, and enduring them, though it does not have the infinite value Christ's endurance had, is still a positive and holy thing.

This was very much the atmosphere of a small book I remember being popular among some Christians when I was a child, entitled *The Joyful Vocation to Suffering*.[2] It nowhere suggested for a moment that God demanded our suffering before he would save or forgive us, nor that we had to make ourselves suffer more than the sufferings life put in our path. But it did propose, as Catholic devotional literature has traditionally done, that our sufferings could be mystically taken up into Christ's and thus share in their redemptive quality. And it might be said that this is the true Catholic doctrine in this matter, even though it has never been formally defined. Provided it is carefully worked out, it is not obviously vulnerable to Luther's criticism.

Yet to me Luther's critique cuts deeper than this. Whatever theory of the Atonement we adopt – and here again the Church has never declared one rather than another to be correct – the idea of Atonement takes as its starting point a certain *givenness* in the work done by Jesus to bring about our salvation. The world in its fallen state is an evil and painful place, for all the signs of joy and goodness it also contains. Christ's death – or rather, Christ's death and resurrection and gift of the Spirit, the whole complex that Catholics nowadays call 'the Paschal mystery' – is God's chosen means to save human beings from the evil and suffering and to give them eternal life: that is, life lived in God's presence and filled with God's joy. The appropriate response to this love cannot – logically cannot – be to seek more suffering. Luther's critique does not challenge just *pathological* religious suffering, it challenges also most forms of asceticism even of a moderate kind – though a strict Lutheran lifestyle can be as ascetic as anything Catholics go in for, as anyone will know if they have seen the film *Babette's Feast*. Luther's theology of the cross sees the cross, as many early Christians did, as a place of triumph: the place where the apparently inevitable connection of humanity with sin and suffering was finally broken, and the prisoners set free. Thereafter, when human beings suffer, their sufferings are not to be seen as sharing in the work of salvation, nor certainly to be scorned as too puny *even* to share in that work – as though, however bad your pain may be, it cannot measure up to what God truly requires, and demonstrates in Christ's sufferings. On the contrary, suffering is simply a sign that Christ's victory is still to become 100 per cent effective on the ground, as it were. Suffering shows that the world, though redeemed, has yet fully to realize the fruits of its redemption. But suffering has no positive value, such that anyone ought to seek it or be glad to have it. When you suffer, God loves you, not your suffering.

This may sound quite negative. Its merit is that it recognizes more fully the once-for-all and decisive character of Christ's atoning work, and that it avoids any glamorizing of suffering. There is no doubt in my mind that there are Christians who do glamorize suffering, whether their own or other people's, and my modern consciousness together with some Lutheran sympathies makes me deeply uneasy about this. The question to ask about suffering is always first and foremost how it can be got rid of. If it cannot – and this is true of much, perhaps the majority of suffering in the world – then the question is how the sufferer can be affirmed as one whom God loves and whose suffering he would like to remove if this were possible. In an imperfect world it may not be possible.

There are positive things, even so, to be said about suffering with Christ, which we shall look at in the next chapter. But we need first to have firmly in our mind that objections to such an idea do not necessarily derive from any anti-Christian sentiments, but arise from within the Christian tradition itself. It is not because our sufferings are too trivial that we should not attempt to 'mingle' them with Christ's. Human sufferings can easily be as great as or even, terrible as it is to contemplate, worse than his. It is no part of Christian belief that Jesus suffered more than anyone else has ever done or can ever do, and the last century devised ways of killing (or just failing to kill) people much more sophisticated in their cruelty even than crucifixion. The sufferings of Jesus on the cross do not save the world because they are the worst, but because of God's involvement in and with them. This is something our own sufferings cannot, but also do not need to, share.

My aim in this chapter has been rather simple: to undermine the idea that suffering is good for you in itself, and that by embracing it deliberately we can have some kind of share in the world's salvation. When suffering strikes, as it does all of us, the Christian tradition has many resources for coping, which will concern us next. But my plea is that this particular way, the idea of 'suffering with Christ', can all too easily lead down a blind alley. In Holy Week, it is common enough for clergy, at least in my own Anglican tradition, to tell their congregations that 'in this week we try to suffer with Christ in his Passion'. This, I believe, is risky. Risky because at the very least the words may strike home to someone who is already afflicted rather pathologically with a desire to suffer; and risky at a deeper theological level because it can compromise the uniqueness of the sufferings of Christ, not in degree but in their link with God's own intervention in our world, which is a belief in which all Christians share. As we shall see, that is not all that can be said about 'walking in the way of the cross', but it is one thing that needs to be said about it. Here in conclusion is an excerpt from a sermon of John Donne (1572–1631), preached when he was Dean of St Paul's Cathedral. Donne emphasizes that there is indeed a cross for each of us to take up, and yet tries, much in Luther's spirit, to discourage us from hunting around until we have found a cross for ourselves and taken care to ensure that it is greater than we can truly bear:

Forraine crosses, other mens merits are not mine; spontaneous and voluntary crosses, contracted by mine own sins, are not mine; neither are devious, and remote, and unnecessary crosses, my crosses. Since I am bound to take up my crosse, there must be a crosse that is mine to take up; that is, a crosse prepared for me by God, and laid in my way, which is tentations or tribulations in my calling; and I must not go out of my way to seeke a crosse; for, so it is not mine, nor laid for my taking up. I am not bound to hunt after a persecution, nor to stand it, and not flye, nor to affront a plague, and not remove, nor to open myself to any injury, and not defend. I am not bound to starve myself by inordinate fasting, nor to teare my flesh by inhumane whippings, and flagellations. I am bound to take up my crosse; and that is onely mine which the hand of God hath laid for me, that is, in the way of my calling, tentations and tribulations incident to that.[3]

1 See Elizabeth Clark, *Theory and Theology in George Herbert's Poetry: 'divinitie and poesie, met'* (Oxford: Oxford University Press, 1997).
2 Edith Barfoot, *The Joyful Vocation to Suffering: intended for invalids and chronic sufferers* (Oxford: Basil Blackwell, 1957).
3 John Donne, Sermon 72 (1619). 'Forraine' (i.e. foreign) here means 'belonging to someone else'.

2. God and Human Suffering

We ended the first chapter with John Donne's idea that there is a cross meant for each of us to bear, but that it is not to be a cross of our own devising. We have no duty to go looking for it, but should let it emerge from the situation in which we find ourselves. Now 'the situation in which we find ourselves' is a vague phrase, and it can well include situations that do indeed call for a heroism which will bring us suffering, and those in which our commitment to others is virtually certain to lead in that direction. The Christians who sheltered Jews on the continent during World War II were not, in Donne's terms, seeking out crosses for themselves, yet their commitment to shared humanity with the victims they took in led them to a decision that might very probably lead them to terrible suffering. Donne was not saying simply that we should play safe. He was trying to argue against the desire of some Christians to invent sufferings for themselves to bear, in a mistaken idea that thereby they would be suffering with Christ.

Suffering is not a precondition of being accepted by God – and if it were, then Christ has done it all for us. But in a world where suffering continually occurs, Christians need to find some way of understanding it. I have been suggesting that understanding it as suffering 'with Christ' may not be the most helpful model. We need a way of thinking that allows a greater place to the fact that most of what we suffer is not and cannot be voluntarily chosen by us, but comes our way in the course of events: 'in the way of my calling ... tentations and tribulations incident to that'. I have been helped towards this by a sermon of Austin Farrer, which I think is broadly in line with Donne's thinking. The 'text', as it were, is the slogan on the side of a florist's van: CROSSES AND WREATHS MADE TO ORDER:

Crosses are never what we ordered, but always either greater than we ordered, smaller than we ordered, or other than we ordered – and it does not matter which; for God measures the love with which they are carried, and not the poundage of each particular weight. Wreaths are never what we ordered, either; but, unlike crosses, the wreaths all have the same fault – they are all ridiculously big and splendid; because God's thoughts are not as our thoughts, and he prepares for man such good things as pass man's understanding. So the wreaths he orders for us throw into the shade all the crosses he assigns us, and it becomes painfully obvious that our crosses will never deserve our crowns. If you want to see a wreath and a cross to match it, you must go as far as the empty sepulchre outside Jerusalem; and there you may see the great garland of glory with, lying beside it, a cross not unworthy of it: a cross which lately stood upright on Calvary, but now is laid beside the crown of fadeless flowers. Look closely at this cross, and there you shall see, like a little jewel laid over the intersection of its arms, whatever cross you have faithfully born for God's sake. Alone, it would not be measurable against the glorious crown; but the great arms of Christ's cross extend the spread of yours, and fit it to the heavenly scale.[1]

This way of thinking is in many ways simpler and less convoluted than the more sophisticated 'suffering with Christ' theology. It is in fact not all that far from what people mean when they say things like 'We all have our cross to bear', or 'I suppose it's just the cross I have to carry'. These phrases can express pure fatalism, and as such are not Christian. But they can also reflect a realism about the world that Christians sometimes lack. If there are Christians who are always looking out for ways of making themselves suffer, there are others who are full of a belief that no true Christian ever does suffer, that suffering is a sign of God-forsakenness. One need only think of the agony some Christians feel if people they believe in as great and faithful believers succumb to sickness or premature death – such was the case some years ago when David Watson, the vicar of St Michael-le-Belfry in York, died of cancer. Against the (often Catholic) culture of suffering in imitation of Christ, there is an opposite (often evangelical and Calvinist) culture that links success, good health, and prosperity to a living faith, and has no resources for coping with obvious exceptions. Like the Psalmist, such people say, 'I have been young, and now am old, yet I have not seen the righteous forsaken, or their children begging bread' (Psalm 37.25). One can only wonder where they have been.

Against that, the everyday, mundane observation that 'we all have our cross to bear' seems to me quite useful and by no means unchristian. The world is not so arranged that faithful Christians escape suffering. There is no 'plan' for them that exempts them from the sufferings everyone else endures, so that 'the Lord looks after his own'. And once it is acknowledged that suffering comes to all of us, the more Catholic idea of suffering with Christ at least makes some sense of it. Is there any alternative way of making sense of suffering if we decide to abandon that way of putting it, or does suffering then become simply a matter of bad luck, from which God and his will for us are absent?

Somehow we need to find a way of saying that suffering can come our way by chance, by bad luck, at random, without denying that God is in it and that through it we can find our way to him. This is far from easy. What is easy is to fall off the tightrope, and lapse either into talking as though God deliberately causes us to suffer and wants us to, rather than rescuing us from suffering, or (on the other hand) that it is our fault when we suffer, because the righteous are never afflicted, so that our suffering proves that we do not really love or trust God. But the truth must lie along the tightrope, and not in these ravines on either side.

To approach some way of putting all this, let me offer two brief case studies. I spoke to two people I know (some details are changed, of course, to avoid recognition), who suffer either chronically or intermittently from, respectively, physical and mental pain, and got them to describe their experience, and their religious understanding of suffering and means of coping with it.

My first friend is a man of 55, whom I'll call Bob. He works in an ironmonger's. Bob has suffered from severe pain in the neck and shoulders for many years. The pain can be treated to some extent, but the basic condition cannot be cured. Though it is not life-threatening, the condition causes complete disruption to normal activities when it comes on, and its course can't be predicted. I asked Bob whether he could use the phrase 'suffering with Christ' to describe his own experience of pain, or whether he could find some other way of putting it that related the experience to his Christian faith. He said he doesn't think of it as suffering with Christ, partly because though the pain is bad he doesn't want to compare it with what Christ suffered on the cross, but also partly because that just is not the kind of vocabulary he uses to himself: his faith comes out in practicalities rather than in theological expressions. He feels more that the pain tends to alienate him from God: he can't pray very easily when he is in pain, and he is so preoccupied with waiting till he can have the next painkiller that nothing beyond that has much hold on his mind. But when he gets better, and starts going to church again, he does for a time have thoughts rather different from his usual thoughts, though they gradually fade as he gets back to normal. These thoughts are concerned with the question of where God was while the pain was so bad. He used to think angrily that God must have gone away, but recently he has come to feel that God was there all the time and somehow shared the pain with him, though he can't be sure that that really means anything. He does not see that the sufferings *of Christ* have anything in particular to do with it, but does think that in some sense there must be something like suffering in God or God wouldn't be able to understand what he is going through, which he is sure God does.

My other friend is a woman in her late thirties, whom I'll call Wendy. Wendy is a hairdresser. She has suffered since her late teens with recurring bouts of severe depression. Her depression comes on more or less without warning and remits, after she has taken the right medication, equally suddenly, but while it is on her she can do very little and certainly cannot work. Because of this rather sudden switch she has the feeling that her life, which the rest of the time is quite happy and cheerful, has periods of what she calls nonsense, in which nothing can be understood. During the depression the recovery which, from experience, she knows rationally is coming, feels quite impossible, and ordinary life becomes severely disrupted. When she is ill the depth of the mental pain and despair is such that thoughts of suicide are never far away, though so far she has never made any attempt to put them into practice.

Asked about the religious significance of it all, Wendy said that the majority of comments made to her by religious people made the depression rather worse. Some diagnose her problem as a lack of trust in God, and this simply endorses one of the elements in her own distorted thinking and helps her to feel that she doesn't deserve to get better. But even leaving such Job's comforters aside, she finds that religious people often do remind her that Christ suffered this sense of abandonment too, and that that should be a comfort to her. When well she can make something of this idea, but when ill, it tends to increase her sense of living in a crazy universe, in which even God's own Son was subject to chaotic experiences and feelings. Like Bob, she said that the best religious answer was that God was somehow or other present even in this experience in which any kind of comfort feels so absent. The idea that she was sharing Christ's sufferings struck her as pretty incomprehensible, but she could get somewhere with the idea that everyone has a cross to bear, including Jesus, including herself, perhaps even including God, whatever that could possibly mean. It isn't sensible, she said, to expect a painless life, and her illness, though severe, was probably no worse than many other people suffered, and at least there were gaps between the episodes. In some ways it probably made her more grateful for the good things in the world than many normal people are, because she knew how horrible it could all seem and how pleasant it was, therefore, when things went right. And times of light and dark alternating seems in some vague way to be how the world is anyway. We get good and bad, and have to take the rough with the smooth. As William Blake put it (this is my gloss on what she said),

> Man was made for Joy and Woe;
> And when this we rightly know,
> Thro' the World we safely go.[2]

These little cameos tell us only what certain people feel they need, not about what the truth is, theologically. Yet

I believe they do point usefully in a certain direction. Neither of these people could make much use of the idea of suffering with Christ; for Bob it was just an unfamiliar way of talking, while Wendy said that when she was ill her picture of herself was so bad that she couldn't begin to think of equating herself with Christ anyway; and when well, she too thought it an inappropriate, over-the-top way of talking. What both of them did find helpful was the idea of Christ, or God through Christ, suffering with *them* – being there when they were in the deep pit which is physical or mental pain. They could get somewhere, not with the idea of our suffering with God, but with the idea of God's suffering with us.

Theologically this is a perilous and potentially an absolutely disastrous idea. Despite Jürgen Moltmann's persuasive work *The Crucified God*,[3] few theologians have thought it wise to set off down the road that leads to talk of God suffering, and that for much the reason that led the early Fathers of the Church to condemn the idea: that, to put it crudely, it leaves no one in charge of the universe. The God who can suffer with me is not a God on whose strength I can rely, but one who is no stronger than I am myself. So theology continues to maintain that though, in Jesus, the Second Person of the Trinity – the eternal Son – suffered and died, the Father is impassible, that is, not able to suffer. To abandon this is to abandon monotheistic religion altogether.

Moltmann developed his ideas about God as the crucified one from the terrible passage from Elie Wiesel's book *Night*,[4] in which he tells of a boy being hanged publicly in Auschwitz, and lasting half an hour in agony.

When someone asked, 'Where is God now?', Wiesel says that he heard a voice saying, 'There he is, on the gallows.' But Moltmann's decision to pick this up and to say that in Christ God hangs on the cross met with furious hostility from Jewish readers, who said, in effect, 'Can Christians not leave us even the Holocaust, that they must be for ever Christianizing even the terrible experiences that belong to Jews alone?' In a way, just as serious an objection is that the boy did die in the end; and Wiesel's inner voice speaks not of God as the one who suffers in our midst in a consoling way, but of the God who, in the wake of Auschwitz, can only be declared finally dead. The story is about the Holocaust as the death of God, not about God suffering with us.

Yet however dangerous an idea the suffering of God may be, Christians persist in feeling that something in it is true and necessary. Wendy reports that in her lowest depression she cannot feel that God is with her. The grey country in which her mind and emotions wander seems to lack all human presence, and all divine presence, too. But in recovery she has a strong sense that God has been there all along, just waiting for the right moment to nudge her back into the real, sunlit world. To say that God is with us and even suffers with us in our suffering is not necessarily to think of him as emptied out to the same extent as we are. It is, however, to think of him as one who can be affected by our suffering, as a human friend can be. As it says in Psalm 139, we cannot go anywhere in the universe where God is not, and his presence sustains us not just because he is strong and powerful, but also – and perhaps more – because there is something in him that corresponds to weakness and suffering in us, some vulnerable spot that assures us our sufferings do not distance us from him, but attach us to him all the more closely. I do not know how to give a theologically coherent account of these ideas, but I very much hope that they are true.

1 Austin Farrer, *Said or Sung: An Arrangement of Homily and Verse* (London: The Faith Press, 1960), p. 25.
2 William Blake, 'Auguries of Innocence', *c.* 1803.
3 Jürgen Moltmann, *The Crucified God: The Cross of Christ as the Foundation and Criticism of Christian Theology* (London: SCM Press, 1974).
4 Elie Wiesel, *Night; Dawn; The Accident: Three Tales* (London: Robson, 1974).

3. God's Plan

There is a radical difference between two sorts of Christian – nowhere registered in any official statements of doctrine, yet permeating the whole way they live and think. It can be described like this. Suppose I get up in the morning, and I want to decide what to do with the day (often this is a luxury, of course, but let's say that on this particular day I do have freedom to choose). There are two approaches to making this kind of decision among Christians.

One approach is to ask what obligations (work-related or other) there are on me that day, what longer-term commitments I have into which the day might fit, whether there is anyone I ought to see because they need my help, and in any case, if it is a free day, what I feel like doing. If some of the courses of action that come into my mind seem morally doubtful, I might weigh them up, and some might eventually be excluded. As a Christian I know I am not supposed to do anything that would actually be sinful, but, let us hope, many of the choices available are morally acceptable. Once all this thinking is finished – and on an average day it probably occupies only a few seconds – I go ahead and do whatever I decide. At the end of the day, if I have this kind of discipline in my life, I may look back and mull over whether what I have done has been well done. I give God thanks for everything that has been good in the day, and put it behind me.

But a completely different scenario is also possible. This is to pray when I get up, not just that I will do right that day (i.e. not do anything morally wrong), but that I will do the *specific* things God wants me to do. I aim not simply to ensure that my actions are good and not evil, but that the *plan* God has for my life may be fulfilled in every particular, as I co-operate with what he has in store for me. For those who see things in this way, the new day is never a tabula rasa on which I can paint in any colours (provided I do not disobey any of God's laws and remain open to the claims of those around me). On the contrary, the day is one page in a life-sized planner, and my task as a Christian is to discern exactly what God has in mind for that page. Of course, God is infinitely resourceful, and can make something even of the mess I make of most of the days he sends me. But it is not an open question for him what I ought to do on each day of my life: he already has something in mind for me, what might be called my vocation for that day.

If you see things in this second way, then your morning prayers are not what a Catholic might call 'remote preparation' for the day ahead, that is, straightening out your will and your intentions so that they are in line with the general standards God sets up for Christians, and so that you are more likely to react in a good way whatever befalls you. Rather, they are an attempt to discern quite specifically what God wants us to do on that particular day. And God has methods for communicating his will to us: through the Scriptures, through particular events or people that we encounter, through silent reflection, through his answer to direct prayers for illumination. Discerning God's will, on this model, does not mean discerning God's general intentions for us and all the human race, but getting our instructions for the day or even the hour ahead, looking for particular providences, signs of the direction God wants to point us in.

Most Christians probably operate with a mixture of these two models. People of the second type do recognize general moral principles, and are not going to be convinced that God is leading them to do something all Christians would regard as wicked. People of the first type do believe that God sometimes calls us to do something very specific, that the fact a task or challenge is staring us in the face can be a clear message from God. Both types can experience a sense of vocation, a belief that God wants them to change their whole way of life because he has some overarching task for them to perform. Christians use the word vocation especially for the call to be ordained, but, particularly in Protestant tradition, one may feel a call to do many things, including, for example, to work in business, and so generate money and employment from which others, too, will benefit. Nevertheless, anyone who knows a lot of Christians will recognize the two types as genuinely different. It is remarkable that this radical difference between equally sincere and committed Christians seldom finds a place in theological discussion, even though it is a distinction that runs right through the majority of Christian churches, both Catholic and Protestant.

This division over an implicit but very living area of belief runs deep, and it produces markedly different styles of Christian discipleship. Can the Bible give us any guidance on which model to prefer? It seems to me that the Bible too speaks with a divided voice on the subject. In the Old Testament, for example, there are books where God's guidance of human history, and of the lives of individuals within it, is so close and detailed that we should surely say he is presented as having a plan. This would be true, for example, of Exodus or Numbers, of some of what is said about history in the prophets, especially perhaps Ezekiel, and in the book of Daniel. In other places, however, God has at most an overall goal to which he would like history to move, but human sin continually thwarts him. This is the case in many of the historical books, down to the end of Kings, where God's desire to give Israel the Promised Land in perpetuity has been so ruined by their continual rebellion that they actually end up by going back to Egypt, in effect undoing the whole painful process by which God's plan was nearly successful but failed in the end. Even there, though, we could say that there was a plan, despite the fact that human sin has partially prevented it from being fulfilled. But the Old Testament taken as a whole is by no means clear about the divine plan, and there are books, such as Proverbs, which think very much in terms of human freedom to choose any course of action, provided it is not sinful.

The New Testament is generally much clearer that God has a plan, which he will bring about whatever people do to interfere with it. A classic example would be Paul's Letter to the Romans, with its reflections in chapters 9 –

11 on how human sinfulness has modified God's plans for the Jewish people and has allowed the Gentiles to enter the plan before the Jews, contrary to the original intentions of the planner. However, the plan will still eventually come to fruition. Although Gentiles are now entering the kingdom ahead of the Jews rather than behind them (which had been the original intention), God has ingeniously modified the plan so that, after the fullness of the Gentiles has been gathered in, the Jews will also come home after all – provoked into obedience by their envy of the already saved Gentiles! This is a complex scheme, but it does not make sense at all unless we start by believing that God has indeed got a quite detailed plan for the whole human race, and has revealed it through the Scriptures (properly understood). Paul himself clearly believed that God was leading him to quite specific tasks in fulfilment of that plan.

Where most Christians are concerned, however – those of us who are sheep rather than shepherds – there is no strong sense in the New Testament that each day has a divine plan. Looking out for particular providential guidance that will show us what God intends for us each day is hard to ground in any particular biblical text. Paul's letters, for example, tend to give very general moral guidance, not advice on discerning what God wants done at any specific moment, though it may well be that the 'prophets' who existed in the churches he founded did give advice on this. Actual examples of specific divine calls tend to be rather dramatic: the choice of Matthias by lot (Acts 1.15–26), Peter's dream revealing how he should behave towards Gentile believers (Acts 10.9–16). They are not very close to you or me praying for guidance for an ordinary day, though they are certainly compatible with it.

Perhaps the most obvious passage in the Bible that appears to deal with the idea of a divine plan behind events is Ecclesiastes 3.1–8, the famous poem about there being 'a time' for everything:

> For everything there is a season, and a time for every
> matter under heaven:
> a time to be born, and a time to die;
> a time to plant, and a time to pluck up what is planted;
> a time to kill, and a time to heal;
> a time to break down, and a time to build up;
> a time to weep, and a time to laugh;
> a time to mourn, and a time to dance;
> a time to throw away stones, and a time to gather
> stones together;
> a time to embrace, and a time to refrain from embracing;
> a time to seek, and a time to lose;
> a time to keep, and a time to throw away;
> a time to tear, and a time to sew;
> a time to keep silence, and a time to speak;
> a time to love, and a time to hate;
> a time for war, and a time for peace.

This evocative passage, rather like Psalm 23, seems to speak to people at all times in their lives, so that I have heard it read both at weddings and at funerals. Its exact meaning is rather elusive, which is why it is so versatile. One way of understanding it is as a great affirmation of the recurring cycles in nature and in human life. Certain kinds of events and opportunities come round in their sequence. This affirmation of the regular order of things is felt by most people to be good news. It encourages patience and fortitude, based on the knowledge that in God's good time all will be for the best.

On the other hand the passage can also be read as a comment on the pointlessness of human activity, and this seems to be endorsed by the final verse (v. 9), which is never read when it is used at rites of passage: 'What gain have the workers from their toil?' Everything comes round on its appointed path, and all the work you do makes not one whit of difference to it. This is specially plausible if we think, as some commentators do, that the passage had an earlier existence as a poem about the cycles of nature but has been incorporated into Ecclesiastes' pessimistic book precisely by the addition of that final verse. People who use it at a wedding would then be in tune with the passage's original, pre-Ecclesiastes meaning, but would be turning their eyes away from the fatalistic, bored attitude that the author or compiler of the finished book wanted to see in it. On this reading the passage buoys us up and makes us feel good about the world and God's ordering of it, only to let us down with a great bump at the end when we realize that these orders in nature go on their way without our being able to influence them in the slightest. This is very much the usual way of thinking in Ecclesiastes, and it may well be that this is how we are meant to read the passage in its final form.

Optimism and pessimism, however, are not the only two possibilities in the interpretation of Ecclesiastes. I should like here to introduce an interpretation by a German theologian, Gerhard Sauter. In his book *The Question of Meaning*, Sauter tries to show that the pattern of events described in Ecclesiastes is far from being deterministic or pre-planned. It neither rejoices that God fixes everything in advance, nor complains that he does so; it does not believe in a divine plan in that sense at all:

> With these pairs of opposites Qoheleth [the Hebrew name for the author of the book] encompasses human life from its beginning – entry into the world – to its end, death. Thus he is not concerned only with the opportunities for decision on which every action depends. Equally, he is not saying that everything that happens is determined, in such a way that one can only accept it as fate. Granted that birth and death are not a matter of decision, planting and weeding are tied to the annual cycle, and the outbreak of war or the conclusion of a peace may well have struck those who belonged to a little nation that had become the plaything of the great powers as blows of fate, beyond their power to alter; still much else, many day-to-day events, were still subject to human choice – and yet at the same time determined.[1]

He goes on to argue that even the activities listed which are genuinely free nevertheless subject those who do them to the constraint that in doing them, their opposite – which they might also want to do – is excluded.

> Our world – the world of our experience and our action – consists of mutually exclusive opposites. In every

action and in every experience the opposite of what gives it its meaning is logically excluded.

Thus, where many commentators see this passage as essentially an expression of 'theological determinism',[2] Sauter prefers to understand it – surely more profoundly – as a reflection on the finite and contingent nature of human existence. One choice always excludes another, and time does not return for us to have a second attempt at making our lives. If there is 'a time to embrace, and a time to refrain from embracing', or 'a time to plant, and a time to pluck up what is planted' (3.5, 2), that is not because God fixes the *destiny* of each thing and controls each of our activities – so that our apparent freedom is a deception, and we are moved around like pieces on a cosmic chessboard. On the contrary, our choices are real choices; but they are subject to the constraint of linearity. Either planting or pulling up may be appropriate at any given moment, but we cannot have both, and the 'cannot' here is logical: no one, not even God, can do opposite things at the same time. To know the *proper* time is to discern which way our choices should be made, a task that requires all our skill and all the wisdom God can give us. It is not a matter of supine fatalism.

Thus Ecclesiastes, the Old Testament book that seems to many to teach a deterministic theology, is perhaps really the best source of insight into that creative use of contingency which is the heart of God's own activity, and the greatest challenge to ours; for he is the great improviser, who is never defeated by any situation and can always bring good out of evil. The challenge to us is to do the same.

Christians, especially those to whom the notion of 'vocation' is important, are likely to doubt whether such a theology does justice to the call of God to each unique individual, to God's providential guidance in their lives, to his guiding hand in the world's history. It is worth noting, though, a common problem where God's action in our lives is understood in terms of vocation. While this can impart an enormous energy to those tasks that are done in supposed fulfilment of the divine call, it can also result in a downgrading of all other human activities, as though God were absent except where we can feel his hand directly upon us. Whereas, for a biblical faith, there are no parts of life from which God is absent:

> Where can I go from your spirit?
>   Or where can I flee from your presence?
> If I ascend to heaven, you are there;
>   if I make my bed in Sheol, you are there.
> If I take the wings of the morning
>   and settle at the farthest limits of the sea,
> even there your hand shall lead me,
>   and your right hand shall hold me fast.
>
>   (Psalm 139.7–10)

We make our choices, and in doing so we demonstrate what Ecclesiastes reminds us of: that every path we choose to walk down excludes innumerable other paths, any one of which might have turned out (and we shall never know) to have led even more directly to God's preferred way for us. But such speculation is useless, and indeed harmful, because it disguises from us that it is in the present – the present to which for good or ill our choices have brought us – that God is actually to be encountered.

1 Gerhard Sauter, *The Question of Meaning: A Theological and Philosophical Orientation* (Grand Rapids: Eerdmans, 1995). This is a translation of *Was heißt: nach Sinn fragen?* (Munich: Chr. Kaiser Verlag, 1982), and the passages quoted are my own translation from this German original.
2 For example, Gerhard von Rad, *Wisdom in Israel* (London: SCM Press, 1972), pp. 263–83.

4. The Meaning of Life

Asking about God's plan for us normally involves surveying our past and casting our minds forward into the future. We find ourselves wondering where God has led us to, where we have resisted, and where we have followed his calling; and also where he wants us to go next, what is his blueprint for the rest of our lives. I have been trying to suggest that there are flaws in this whole way of thinking, partly for the reasons that we find expressed in Ecclesiastes. Our past is what it is, and can no longer be changed. And our future depends not on one decision, but on a whole host of piecemeal decisions whose most obvious characteristic is their mutual incompatibility. To experiment with one apparently good course of action is to rule out not only bad ones that might mistakenly have been chosen, but also many perhaps equally good or better ones. We cannot go back and try again. Our life is always going to be full of the experience T. S. Eliot refers to:

> Footfalls echo in the memory
> Down the passage which we did not take
> Towards the door we never opened.[1]

But the trouble is that if we take seriously this observed reality, whereby we can only act in a linear way in the light of all past actions, then to have a very high doctrine of God's plan for us means that, with the best of intentions, our life can go completely and disastrously wrong because of one false choice. Whereas if the will of God for us is, rather, that we should make good and wise choices out of a large range of possible options, many of which are perfectly good in themselves, then we can be more relaxed about the whole pattern of our lives. We may make less than ideal choices, but so long as we are not making sinful ones, there is nothing with which to reproach ourselves. We shall not have failed to do the single thing God wanted us to do, because there was no such single thing: he gave us a range of options among which we chose freely. If we think of God as having one, and only one, pattern for our life that he wants us to follow, then there is in each situation only one good choice, and all the others are wrong: to misjudge what is the will of God for us today is potentially to throw away our whole life. This is why I said at the end of the last chapter that a strong sense of vocation can impart a great energy to the tasks we do in fulfilment of it, but can also result in a downgrading of all other activities. They become either neutral and of no interest to God, or (more likely) they are seen as tainted with sin because they do not contribute to the fulfilment of the one thing he wants us to do. That way lies a lot of unhappiness, not to say despair, if we think we have missed our vocation. We have all known people in the grip of a single great mission which may have been admirable in itself, but led them to neglect ordinary human relationships and daily obligations as beneath their notice. It is other people who suffer from their single-mindedness.

If I have made my point, you may think that it should make us very cagey about saying our choices have anything to do with God at all. That, however, is not the conclusion I am trying to suggest. I began this chapter by pointing out that talk of a divine plan inevitably concerns our past and our future as well as our present. The problem with that is that it can deflect us from the task of living in the present. But the present is the place where God is actually to be encountered and served. If (using the language of Ecclesiastes) we ask about the proper or correct time for our actions, then we soon realize that it is always in the present moment that we meet with God. The present is always the 'proper time' – this present in which we often refuse to live, and from which we tend to hide by musing about the past or imagining the future. This was pointed out by Blaise Pascal, as Sauter reminds us:

We never live in the present. We anticipate the future, as though it were coming too slowly, and we wanted to speed it up; or we remember the past, to make it stay with us, because it disappears too fast. But it is folly to wander around in times which are not ours, and to forget the one time that actually belongs to us; and it is in vain that we yearn for the times that have no existence, while losing the one time that exists, because it is the present which is usually what wounds us ... In this way we never live, but hope to live, and it becomes unavoidable that in our preparations for being happy one day, we never really are.[2]

To treat the present as our place of encounter with God is not to deny or hide from the past, nor is it to be careless of the future consequences of our action. It is to practise what J. P. de Caussade called 'the sacrament of the present moment',[3] in the realization that 'now is the acceptable time ... now is the day of salvation' (2 Corinthians 6.2): now, when we can do something about it; not in the past, which can no longer be mended, nor in the future, which as yet is outside our control.

Perhaps our two types of Christian could find some reconciliation here. Those who believe strongly in the vocational character of each day might try to remember that God continually gives us fresh chances for discipleship; and those who do not naturally think in terms of a divine plan at all might try to see that each day's decisions do at least add up to a *pattern* of response to God, even if not quite to a plan.

A related issue which may help us to break down divisions is the issue of *meaning*. The book of Gerhard Sauter from which I've been quoting is called *The Question of Meaning*. Christians do indeed often talk of their faith as giving meaning to their life or making sense of it. That is a natural and good thing to say: Christian life is not aimless, but directed to God, and that can impart a sense of direction which non-believers sometimes do not have. But Sauter points out, I think importantly, that the idea of a meaning or sense for our lives can be thought of in two different ways, only one of which really does justice to Christian experience and, in fact, to what God has shown us of himself in the Bible and through Jesus Christ.

The definition of the present only in terms of past and future, never itself as the place of encounter with God, is closely related to the question of meaning. Like Ecclesiastes or indeed all the biblical writers, we desperately want the present moment of our life to 'make sense'. But where *they* see this as achieved through the fact that the present moment comes to us from God, is filled with God, and has its unique place in God's (to us unknown) purposes for us and for the world, *we* tend to seek meaning by peering forward, far into the future, and back over our shoulders into the past, straining to see a meaning in the whole historical process which we can identify as God's 'plan' for it, and for us. To 'make sense' or be meaningful to us, it seems, history (world history on the large scale, our own history on the small one) has to 'have a meaning', that is, one specific meaning.

But this desire to discover 'the meaning of life' amounts, Sauter argues, to a desire for self-justification. Christians are not sent on a quest for life's meaning. 'Meaning' in that sense lies beyond human sight, and is a secret that lives only with God. The danger is that in looking into the distance to discover it we shall overlook the present demands – and the present promises – of God, which lie before us. God himself, as the Old Testament hints, does not always act 'meaningfully', if that implies 'according to a plan'. He does not have a fixed schedule of events that he contrives to bring about. For God works in partnership with his creatures, and their ability to change the course of events by their free choices is not an illusion. God is infinitely resourceful, not infinitely in control. How a mere created being can share in shaping God's designs for the world is utterly mysterious, yet the Bible attests that this is what God is like. Contingent choices are as much part of the raw material of his actions as they are of ours.

A biblical 'doctrine of the proper time' was incomparably expressed in another sermon by John Donne:

God made Sun and Moon to distinguish seasons, and day, and night, and we cannot have the fruits of the earth but in their seasons: But God hath made no decree to distinguish the seasons of his mercies; In paradise, the fruits were ripe, the first minute, and in heaven it is always Autumne, his mercies are ever in their maturity. We ask *panem quotidianum*, our daily bread, and God never sayes you should have come yesterday, he never sayes you must again to morrow, but *to day if you will heare his voice*, to day he will heare you. If some King of the earth have so large an extent of Dominion, in North, and South, as that he hath Winter and Summer together in his Dominions, so large an extent East and West, as that he hath day and night together in his Dominions, much more hath God mercy and judgement together: He brought light out of darknesse, not out of a lesser light; he can bring thy Summer out of Winter, though thou have no Spring; though in the wayes of fortune, or understanding, or conscience, thou have been benighted till now, wintred and frozen, clouded and eclipsed, damped and benumbed, smothered and stupefied till now, now God comes to thee, not as in the dawning of the day, not as in the bud of the Spring, but as the Sun at noon to illustrate all shadows, as the sheaves in harvest, to fill all penuries, all occasions invite his mercies, and all times are his seasons.[4]

'All times are his seasons' because at every moment there is a meaningful choice available to us. So long as we persist in thinking of meaning as *the* meaning of our life, our destiny or vocation, there are bound to be occasions when it will seem that nothing 'meaningful' can be done, because like an actor we are 'resting' between two phases of our career. But if we take meaningfulness to imply worthwhileness, appropriateness, that which is 'indeed right, our duty and our joy', we shall not run the risk of dividing our life into polar opposites, with a huge weight of meaning attaching to some parts and no meaning at all to others. There are peaks and troughs in any life, but the steady, day-by-day activity that underlies both is the place where meaning is to be located. Seeking one's destiny or vocation is all very well; but if that is the only way to finding meaning in life, what hope is there for the 99 per cent of people who have no choice in such matters? Yet for them, too, life can surely be meaningful – but only if 'meaning' is not linked so inseparably to the pursuit of some goal that is only available to those with free choice about how to spend their day, or their life.

Gerhard Sauter shows that there have been two approaches to the question of meaning among those who have concerned themselves most with the human perception of the world and our place in it, such as psychologists and counsellors who have taken on the task of helping us to understand ourselves. Jung's psychology, which is widely influential in Britain especially among clergy, is on the whole in favour of the question of 'the meaning of life'. For Jung, a neurosis was the suffering of a soul that had not discovered its own meaning, or the meaning of its life. One goal of therapy was integration, which makes the person being counselled able to embrace a holistic view of the world, and so give an account of the meaning of his or her place within it.

But Freud took the opposite view. He wrote in a letter, 'As soon as someone starts to ask about the meaning and value of life, they are ill.'[5] The healthy person, for Freud, is not someone who has pondered the question of meaning and won through to a correct interpretation of the world, but someone who finds such satisfaction and meaningfulness in their daily life that such agonized questions do not arise in their mind in the first place. The role of religion is not to provide answers to questions that healthy and well-adjusted people don't ask anyway. It is to stimulate thankfulness to God for the sense that daily surrounds us, and moral obedience to his will – meaning here not 'the plan he has drawn up for our life' but 'the good choices he wants us to make in whatever situation we find ourselves'. It does seem to me that Freud's attitude to the question of meaning is the sounder one. It is not our task to discover what plan God has for the universe, or even for ourselves, and if we think it is, we shall fritter our lives away worrying at unanswerable questions. It is our task to accept from God's hand the choices and opportunities that each moment gives us, to rejoice in being able to respond in a way that is meaningful, that is, not aimless or pointless.

Wendy, my depressive friend, helped me to see this more clearly. She said that during her depression she is continually gnawed at by the feeling that there is no meaning in life, and by an absolute certainty that it is only when she discovers that meaning that she will recover. In the past some religious friends have fed this feeling, telling her that she will indeed only get better when she discovers what God's special purpose for her is. There's not a lot of chance that someone afflicted with a depressive illness will come to any very sensible answers to that question, and the impossibility of doing so thus confirms her in her depressed state, cruelly enough. But when she recovers, it is not because she *has* discovered the meaning and purpose of her existence; what happens is that the question immediately ceases to be very interesting. There is too much to enjoy, too many happy days to live through in a constructive way, to torture herself with questions about the meaning of life. What looked to her and her friends like a cause of the depression – a failure to identify God's plan and to see the meaning of her existence – turns out, when the depression remits, to have been part of the depression itself (just as Freud said), and it disappears like a puff of smoke.

Wendy is keen on knitting, but when depressed she stops doing it, thinking all the time that it has no point, achieves nothing, gets you nowhere. But it's not the case that she eventually remembers or discovers what the point is, and is thereby released from her depression. What happens is that she suddenly realizes, on emerging from the illness, that it does not have to have a point, but is simply a good activity that is its own justification. After all, we are not told in Genesis for what point God made the world or what its meaning was, but that does not mean his creative activity was point*less* or aimless. The world was indeed 'very good'. He had knitted it himself.

1 T. S. Eliot, *Four Quartets: Burnt Norton* (1935).

2 Gerhard Sauter, *Was heißt: nach Sinn fragen* (Munich: Chr. Kaiser Verlag, 1982), p. 34, quoting Pascal, *Pensées*, p. 172; my own translation.

3 J. P. de Caussade, *The Sacrament of the Present Moment* (Glasgow: Collins; London: Fount Paperback 1981). De Caussade died in 1751.

4 John Donne, *Eight Sermons*, 1640: Sermon 2; preached in St Paul's on Christmas Day 1624.

5 S. Freud, *Briefe 1873–1939* (Frankfurt am Main: S. Fischer, 1960), p. 429; quoted in Sauter, *Was heißt*, pp. 20, 174.

5. Ministering to Others

'Ministry' in a Christian context often suggests ordained ministry. But in recent decades it has become much commoner to suggest that all Christians should exercise a ministry towards others, and it's in that sense that I shall be using the word here. We have come to see that every Christian has a role in being not only, as it were, a sheep, but also a shepherd. Quite apart from any considerations of ordination or authorization in the Church, it belongs to the task of everyone to care and look out for fellow-Christians, and indeed everyone with whom life brings them into contact. There are naturally times in all of our lives when we shall be ministered to rather than actively ministering, and there are situations, often including some situations in the work-place, where ministry in any overt sense can be inappropriate; but in our personal relationships with others we all have the duty (and the privilege) of being channels for the love of God to flow out on those around us, and this can well be called a form of ministry. This again is an area in which there are no formal definitions in any of the churches. Each church tends to have very tight rules about who can and cannot serve in *ordained* ministry, but on the question of each Christian's daily ministry to others we are again in the realm of implicit rather than explicit belief, and yet, again, near the heart of many people's living faith.

I am going to suggest that the practice of Christian ministry to others requires a careful balance of two apparently opposing qualities, empathy and detachment. It is obvious that one cannot minister to others without some degree of empathy with them, though we have probably all been on the receiving end of attempts to do just that. The popular image of the clergy is notoriously one of people who are entirely out of touch with those they attempt to minister to, and laypeople who take on any formal ministerial role in the churches are often assumed to be similarly remote from ordinary life. The image of the vicar in *Dad's Army*, an ineffective buffoon, pervades the media's idea of Christian ministry. Effective ministry, however, clearly involves a deep understanding of people and an ability to get alongside them, and that is the kind of thing I mean by using the word empathy.

It is sometimes assumed that Christian ministry comes into its own in times of trouble and disaster. Of course it is at such times that people often look to others in the Church, both ordained and lay, for comfort and support. But it is worth remembering that the commitment of Christians to others is summed up in the formula 'rejoice with those who rejoice, weep with those who weep' (Romans 12.15), and that rejoicing here comes before weeping. The image of the Christian priest as the one who appears on the horizon only when there has been a death is a misleading one, contributing to the idea that we do not need the ministry of others except when things go badly wrong. In most Christian churches, after all, an appointed minister is there, too, at times of rejoicing, notably at marriages and baptisms, times when we celebrate new beginnings, joy, not sorrow. The practice of ministering to others is not typically defined in terms of supporting them in difficulties, but of being alongside them at all times, most especially including times of happiness. One of the pleasures of ordained ministry is certainly having a role when people have cause for rejoicing, but this is a pleasure that does not have to be limited to the ordained; everyone can enjoy the happiness of others, and those who do not enjoy seeing other people flourishing and contented are unlikely to be of much use to them in times of hardship.

There are people involved in full-time ministry who suffer from what is sometimes called co-dependency: to put it crudely, they need us to have problems so that they can help to sort them out. The co-dependent person is at a loose end when other people are happy, drawing strength only from their misery because then there is a role to fulfil as helper and alleviator. They need our troubles as much as we need them to get us out of them. Those who recruit for all the 'caring professions' are always warily on the lookout for the co-dependent personality, in which the empathetic, and commendable, human desire to help others takes on a slightly pathological tinge. C. S. Lewis once spoke memorably of someone who lived for others 'and you can always tell the others by their hunted expression'.[1]

The test of whether someone will minister well is not only whether they show concern for people in distress –

for co-dependent people do that too – but whether they show joy in other people's happiness. Good ministers are happiest when they are in a sense not needed, or rather when they are needed to help the party along, because they are supremely good at helping others to rejoice. They know the particular pleasure that comes to those who assist other people so well that they themselves eventually become in a sense redundant, a pleasure well known to 'enablers' of every kind, in management, in education, in parenting. A good 'minister' enjoys the moment when they can say 'You don't need my help any longer': 'I crown and mitre you over yourself', as Virgil says to Dante in *The Divine Comedy* at the point where he is no longer needed as a guide.[2] Those who cannot understand this kind of pleasure should beware of getting too deeply into 'helping' other people.

Being empathetic, then, does not mean simply agonizing with others, but being able to enter into all their states of mind and feeling, including the good ones. But it also includes knowing what it is like to have human weaknesses, knowing what it is to be sinful. This means that empathizing with others requires us to have some insight into our own depths, bad as well as good. I stumbled on a vivid description of this kind of empathy, when I was too young to understand it, through an addiction to detective novels. Like many teenagers of my generation I was keen on Sherlock Holmes, who appeals to young minds because he solves all his crimes by the power of pure logic, with a kind of mathematical technique: not surprising that he appeals so much to the autistic narrator in Mark Haddon's *The Curious Incident of the Dog in the Night-time*[3] (itself a quotation from a Holmes story, 'Silver Blaze'), who does not understand human emotion but is supremely good at solving puzzles. But Sherlock Holmes led me on to G. K. Chesterton's Father Brown, an amateur detective of a very different stamp. Father Brown uses an approach exactly opposite to that of Holmes. He solves crimes by means of something we might now call psychological profiling, imagining what it would be like to commit the crime in question. Here is his own description of his method (which is not a method at all) in the story 'The Secret of Father Brown'. An American visitor has asked how he manages to solve so many crimes, and at first Brown refuses to be drawn, but when the visitor suggests it was probably by occult means he cannot remain silent and has to attempt an explanation:

'The secret is,' he said; and then stopped as if unable to go on. Then he began again and said:

'You see, it was I who killed all those people.'

'What?' repeated the other, in a small voice out of a vast silence.

'You see, I had murdered them myself,' explained Father Brown patiently. 'So, of course, I knew how it was done.'

'I had planned out each of the crimes very carefully,' went on Father Brown, 'I had thought out exactly how a thing like that could be done, and in what style or state of mind a man could really do it. And when I was quite sure that I felt exactly like the murderer myself, of course I knew who he was.'

[The American] gradually released a sort of broken sigh.

'You frightened me all right,' he said. 'For the minute I really did think you meant you were the murderer ... Why, of course, if it's just a figure of speech and means you tried to reconstruct the psychology —— '

Father Brown rapped sharply on the stove with the short pipe he was about to fill; one of his very rare spasms of annoyance contracted his face.

'No, no, no,' he said, almost angrily; 'I don't mean just a figure of speech ... I mean that I really did see myself, and my real self, committing the murders. I didn't actually kill the men by material means; but that's not the point. Any brick or bit of machinery might have killed them by material means. I mean that I thought and thought about how a man might come to be like that, until I realized that I really *was* like that, in everything except actual final consent to the action. It was once suggested to me, by a friend of mine, as a sort of religious exercise. I believe he got it from Pope Leo XIII.'

[He continued,] 'I try to get inside the murderer ... Indeed, it's much more than that, don't you see? I *am* inside a man. I am always inside a man, moving his arms and legs; but I wait until I know I am inside a murderer, thinking his thoughts, wrestling with his passions; till I have bent myself into the posture of his hunched and peering hatred; till I see the world with his bloodshot and squinting eyes, looking between the blinkers of his half-witted concentration; looking up the short and sharp perspective to a pool of blood. Till I really am a murderer.'

'Oh,' said [the American], regarding him with a long, grim face, and added, 'And that is what you call a religious exercise.'

'Yes,' said Father Brown; 'that is what I call a religious exercise.'[4]

Chesterton hit on something important here. Probably this isn't a good method for solving crime, but it certainly is a religious exercise. Being a minister to others is simply a way of being human, and being human means sharing certain capacities for good and evil. Those who exercise a ministry towards others need to be sharply aware of these capacities in themselves, and perhaps especially the capacity for evil. If you are a person others confide in, you will sometimes hear shocking things. You will be ineffective as a minister if your reaction is nothing but shock, and if you think at once 'I can't imagine how anyone could ever do that.' On the contrary, you need to be able to understand only too easily how anyone could, because you know you have it in yourself.

Of course there are actions that are genuinely shocking, and we can only open our minds so far – we are limited not only by our experience but also by our capacity for imagination. But we need to recognize within ourselves something that, if allowed to develop, could result even in the evil we're hearing about. We can practise this skill in the manner of Father Brown, by thinking not only about people we know but about actions, including crimes, reported in the media or read about in novels. The daily news offers plenty of material for reflection. I have also found yet another set of detective novels, those of Ruth Rendell, useful for providing pictures of people with distorted personalities that it is worth trying to get inside. The crucial thing is to make ourselves aware what vast reserves we have in us of deceitfulness, malice, resentment, hatred, and selfishness. This kind of imaginative participation in other people's wickedness really is a form of religious exercise for anyone trying to minister to others, in effect a form of confession.

Imagination of this sort is not the only spiritual resource in ministering to others. In any case, if we really do commit a crime, we shall probably feel quite differently about it from what is being described here. But the value of the exercise is that it forces you to consider what it would be like to look out on the world through someone else's eyes. We need some way of trying to take into ourselves the temptations and trials, the pleasures and pains, of other people's lives, so that we can indeed 'rejoice with those who rejoice, and weep with those who weep'. This is hard. Those who wish to minister to others have to try not to find their fellow human beings revolting, intolerable, hateful, or unimaginable; and their reaction to what other people feel needs not to be one of shock and horror, but of understanding and compassion. That is impossible unless we are aware of the horrible things that go on in ourselves, often below the level of our deliberate intentions – things that come into our minds when we're not thinking of anything in particular. No one has an unlimited imagination, and the ability to be shocked is itself a valuable one, which acts as a moral guard on human action; but lowering our threshold of shockability can certainly be a positive contribution to making us better able to minister to others.

Thus empathy is essential for any kind of ministry to others. The Anglican tradition of pastoral care has always been slanted in this direction. In it clergy themselves are not seen as special religious operatives flown into a parish to carry out a kind of religious commando operation, but as people who live alongside their parishioners and share their life experiences to the full. The rejection of clerical celibacy as a universal requirement (it may be part of a personal vocation) has been part of that tradition: it implies that clergy should be open to the many experiences and tensions that face their people. Of course it means also that they are not protected from the many complications of sexual attraction, jealousy, and infidelity. But the sense of being part of the culture of those among whom they live and work has been an important part of the self-image of Anglican clergy.

There is of course a corresponding weakness – too little detachment. This I shall discuss in the next chapter. The sense of total immersion in the culture in which one ministers can blunt the prophetic edge of the Church's voice and leave it unable to criticize the society in which it is set. And there can be little doubt that this has happened to Anglicanism in many periods. It was one of the criticisms levelled by early Methodists, for example, and not only early ones: Nonconformists and Roman Catholics alike complain that the Church of England is compromised in its witness by too cosy a relationship with society. Properly practised, however, an empathetic ministry need not lead to collusion and collaboration, any more than Father Brown's empathy for murderers actually leads him to murder. What it does exclude is the kind of 'prophetic' ministry that simply does not see the difficulties faced by those it challenges, and is essentially utopian. An awareness that we who minister are ourselves also fully human, not exempt from the difficulties and temptations all human beings face, can be part of an effective evangelism, not a barrier to it. Christians, including Christian ministers, need to be perceived as human first, otherwise the good news they preach will seem like a message only for superhumans and will go unheard. Being Christian is one way of being human, not a substitute for it.

1 C. S. Lewis, *The Screwtape Letters* (1942), No. 25 (London: Fount Paperbacks, 1982).
2 Dante, *Purgatorio* xxvii.142.
3 Mark Haddon, *The Curious Incident of the Dog in the Night-time* (London: Jonathan Cape, 2003).
4 G. K. Chesterton, *The Father Brown Stories* (London: Cassell, 1960), pp. 464–6.

6. A Foot in Two Worlds

In trying to show how vital empathy is for anyone who wants to minister to others, I also warned that there is the need for a degree of detachment. One of the criticisms sometimes levelled at Anglican approaches to pastoral practice is that they involve too great an identification with the society in which the Church is set, and too little detachment from it. For ordinary Christians who seek to minister to others by the way they live, there is similarly a line to be observed between being simply another friendly face, and therefore doing little that could be called 'witnessing' to the gospel (though in many situations friendly faces are in small enough supply, after all), and representing something that transcends the particular setting in which they are placed. This sense of transcendence is also essential, however much people can exaggerate it and come to seem remote and unreal. Christians in ministering to other people do so as representatives of Jesus Christ; they are not simply trying to spread a good impression of themselves as nice people. So an element of detachment is called for, despite the risks.

In the previous chapter I recalled a story I read in my teens, 'The Secret of Father Brown'. Now I shall turn to another work I encountered at a slightly later age when I studied it for 'A' level German, Thomas Mann's short novel *Tonio Kröger*, published in 1903.[1]

This is a short and more or less autobiographical story. Like Mann himself, the hero grows up in Lübeck in the north of Germany. His father – again like Mann's – belongs to one of the leading families in the city, a major commercial centre, once part of the Hanseatic League (and a beautiful place, too little known by people in Britain). But his mother is Italian, and is called Consuela. Italy seemed exotic to north German citizens in 1903, and the family always refers to her as coming 'from the bottom of the map', wrinkling its collective nose. It is because of her that the hero receives his name Tonio, which carries a considerable stigma in a town where other boys are called Hans or Heinrich or Jürgen. Italy represents the suspicious, sensual south, a place of people with an 'artistic' temperament far removed from the respectabilities of north German life. The novel is concerned with the tension between the staid lives of north European Protestant solid citizens on the one hand, and the free life of the spirit associated with the south on the other.

Tonio spends many years down in Munich, just as Mann did himself. Munich, far in the south of Germany, represents a kind of uneasy compromise. Tonio becomes a novelist, the epitome of an 'artist', yet he always wears the dark suit and tie that go with his family's solid middle-class status. He indulges in what are coyly described as 'adventures of the flesh', yet he constantly reminds himself that he is, after all, 'not a gypsy in a caravan' (a recurring phrase or leitmotiv in the book), but a member of one of Lübeck's most respectable families. Above all, he knows that as an artist, a writer, he must observe the world with detachment, yet as a man he yearns to be immersed in ordinary bourgeois life with an honest nine-to-five job. Unlike most artistic people, as Mann sees them, he does not despise and hate the ordinary people around him as Philistines, but loves them. But unlike these ordinary people themselves, he cannot simply rest in and enjoy normal everyday life, because his need to analyse and describe this life as an uncommitted observer gives him no peace. He becomes a kind of hybrid, a cross between bourgeois solid citizen and detached, ironic artist, constantly oscillating between the two poles and fully at home with neither.

It may be that this combination of detachment and commitment is simply a typical adolescent feeling, at an age when you don't yet know where you belong in the world, and that this is why *Tonio Kröger* resonated with me when I first studied it. But it has stayed with me as containing a lot of wisdom for anyone who seeks to minister to others as a Christian, and it is this aspect I should like to develop here.

Anyone who sees their life as containing elements of ministry to other people must, as we have seen, be immersed in the world they live in. Unless they share the same feelings and experiences as others, they will never be effective in standing alongside them in solidarity and so in supporting and encouraging them in all aspects of their lives. At the same time, there is also a vital need to be able to stand back from this shared world and to criticize it in the name of the gospel, recalling it to insights it would never generate itself, since the gospel (as Paul reminds us in Galatians) does not come from a human source, but from God. Both sides of this are equally important. Christians who look down on the mass of unredeemed humanity all around them are like the cold-hearted 'artists' Tonio Kröger admires in a way, but can never be himself. Yet those who retain no sense of distance from the world at all are like the solid bourgeois people from whom he is partly alienated: like those eighteenth-century clergy who were nothing more than part of the local gentry, and who could offer no critique of the society around them at all.

People who minister in the name of Christ need a precise mixture of attachment and detachment, and this is always potentially painful. It is easy to be simply a 'professionally' religious person, who despises ordinary people. I certainly know clergy who would fit that description. There are also lay people who seem to live in a kind of religious ghetto, never mixing with non-Christians if they can avoid it, and fearing a kind of contamination from the secular world. This is a particular characteristic of some Christian students, and there are churches that encourage them in their ghettoization. It is also easy to be an ordinary secular person, who despises the religious, seeing them as charlatans or hypocrites: this is how much of the media currently perceives Christians. It is very hard to be a committed Christian and an ordinary person at the same time, and in the process to despise nobody. The exact balance is almost impossible to achieve, the more so as it makes you vulnerable on *both* flanks, at home nowhere yet living everywhere. In Tonio Kröger's world, pure literary artists have no difficulty in loving others of their own kind, and ordinary bourgeois people have none in loving those of theirs. But Tonio, this awkward hybrid, loves both, with a strange and slightly contorted love which is reciprocated by neither.

But there are tasks for which a kind of dual citizenship is essential. It was this that contributed in great measure to the genius of Thomas Mann himself, and I believe it contributes similarly to the work of many creative artists. Rootedness in the everyday world along with an ability to observe that world as if from afar makes a combination to which much art is indebted. And my concern here is that a similar creative tension can be crucial in the spiritual work of ministering to other people in the name of Christ. Only a person with one foot in another world can minister the love of God to God's people; but only someone with one foot firmly inside this one has the commitment to other people to want to do so. This is not a melancholy vocation, but a joyful one: it's just that the joy is not simple and uncomplicated. Mann describes it supremely well at the end of the story, where Tonio writes from the north to a friend in Munich in these words:

> I stand between two worlds, and I'm at home in neither, and consequently life can be a little difficult. You artists call me bourgeois, while genuinely bourgeois people try to arrest me [this refers to a comic incident earlier in the story]. I don't know which of the two is more painful. You do not realize that for my kind of art there is no

yearning deeper than the yearning for the pleasures of ordinary life. I have a certain admiration for proud, cold artists who despise ordinary mortals – but I don't envy them. All warmth, all goodness, all humour comes from these ordinary people, and it almost seems to me that it is the love for them of which it is said that someone might speak with the tongues of men and of angels, but if he has not love, he is a sounding brass or a tinkling cymbal … Do not condemn this love; it is good, and fruitful. In it there is much longing, a kind of melancholy envy, and a tiny touch of condescension; but a vast, pure happiness.

To function well in ministering to other people one needs to feel in the same way that despite hardships and misunderstandings, this is a good course to be set on. The call to minister, which is the call all Christians receive at their baptism, does always involve a dual citizenship: our citizenship is in heaven yet we still live on earth. And living on earth can be difficult for Christians. In some places it can involve persecution, but in modern British society it entails being on the receiving end of a certain measure of superior contempt, which we have to be sure we do not reciprocate. Christians have to love the society that marginalizes them. They have to care deeply for all the infuriating people who misunderstand them, and to recognize that they themselves have broader horizons because of their faith, yet without feeling patronizing towards the people who do not share it. They have to be in the world without being of it, yet in such a way that they are really in it, not just pretending.

Their detachment is essential, yet it must never result in a feeling of superiority.

How are we thus to live with both empathy and detachment? It may sound like an intolerable position to be in, but in reality, from day to day, it can be lived with perfectly well. I suggested in the previous chapter that the solidarity or empathy between those who minister and those to whom they minister begins, not in sharing suffering, but in sharing occasions of rejoicing. And it is here that we can find a recipe for a fruitful relation between detachment and empathy. In sharing with those who rejoice, the Christian who ministers is affirming the goodness of ordinary life yet also seeing in it signs of a divine dimension, and helping others, too, to see those signs. In helping people to celebrate their wedding, for example – in which the whole congregation, not just the officiant, has a ministerial function – all those present can rejoice in its capacity to open up new vistas, to suggest hints of transcendence, of something more than what is merely human. Those present who are religious believers see this extra dimension as linked with God. We believe that any God worth believing in is one who affirms and delights in the human flourishing of which a happy marriage is one of the best examples. In committing themselves to getting married in the presence of such a God, people declare that they are open to the possibility that their love for each other will be endorsed by that God, and so will be enabled to flow out beyond themselves to cause others to flourish too. To assist in the celebration of marriage is thus to join together things earthly and things heavenly, in such a way that the tension between empathy and detachment finds a happy resolution.

The resolution can be seen, in fact, in all occasions of thanksgiving, in which what Mann calls 'a vast, pure happiness' can be felt even – or perhaps especially – by the citizens of two worlds we've been discussing. Giving thanks is the central act in the central Christian form of worship, the Eucharist (Greek for thanksgiving). Its core prayer begins 'It is not only right, it is our duty and our joy, at all times and in all places *to give you thanks*, holy Father, heavenly King, Almighty and eternal God.' Those who pray this prayer acknowledge that they live in two worlds, for what they are doing is to take elements of this world, bread and wine, and set them before God as the potential vehicles by which God from his own realm will impart his blessing to them and to all people. And the route from the one world to the other lies through thanksgiving.

Thanksgiving is an activity which, like love according to 1 Corinthians 13, can endure when other activities have fallen away, because it is not related to getting other things done. It is not a means to an end, but an end in itself. Feeling thankful needs no further justification, and when we thank another person we are not aiming at an ulterior purpose (or shouldn't be), but are simply acknowledging how satisfactory our relationship with them already is in respect of the thing we give thanks for. According to Psalm 34, thanking and praising God are something we should do 'at all times'. This is a statement about how everyone's life should be lived, but it is specially relevant to people who seek to minister to others, who need to give thanks for and with and on behalf of them and so to bridge the gap created between humankind and

God by human alienation. Thanksgiving is the great bridge between the worlds.

The centrality of thanksgiving is well expressed by two scholars who have written about the Eucharist. One is the liturgist Gregory Dix, writing in 1945:

The eucharist is not a mere symbolic mystery representing the right order of earthly life, though it is that incidentally and as a consequence. It is the representative act of a fully *redeemed* human life. This perfected society is not an end in itself, but is consciously and wholly directed to the only end which can give meaning and dignity to human life – the eternal God and the loving and conscious human obedience of man in time to His known will. There the eternal and absolute value of each individual is affirmed by setting him in the most direct of all earthly relations with the eternal and absolute Being of God ... There the only means to that end is proclaimed and accepted and employed – man's redemption through the personal sacrifice of Jesus Christ at a particular time and place in human history, communicated to us at other times and places through the church which is the 'fulfilment' of him. That is the eucharist. Over against the dissatisfied 'Acquisitive Man' and his no less avid successor the dehumanized 'Mass-Man' of our economically focussed societies insecurely organized for time, christianity sets the type of 'Eucharistic Man' – man giving thanks with the product of his labours upon the gifts of God, and daily rejoicing with his fellows in the worshipping society which is grounded in eternity. This is man to whom it was promised on the night before Calvary that he should henceforth eat and drink at the table of God … That is not only a more joyful and more humane ideal. It is the divine and only authentic conception of the meaning of all human life.[2]

Dix here presents eucharist – thanksgiving – as the central act of all human life, as the one thing that truly unites us to God and removes our alienation from the life of God.

This theme is taken further, and also stated more simply, in a great book from the 1960s by the Russian Orthodox theologian Alexander Schmemann, *The World as Sacrament*. Schmemann writes:

When man stands before the throne of God, when he has fulfilled all that God has given him to fulfill, when all sins are forgiven, all joy restored, then there is nothing left for him to do but to give thanks. Eucharist (thanksgiving) is the state of perfect man. Eucharist is the life of paradise. Eucharist is the only full and real response of man to God's creation, redemption and gift of heaven … In and through … Eucharist the whole creation becomes what it always was to be and yet failed to be.

'It is fitting and right to give thanks,' answers the congregation, expressing in these words that 'unconditional surrender' with which 'true religion' begins. For faith is not the fruit of intellectual searching. It is not a reasonable solution to the frustrations and anxieties of life. It does not arise out of a 'lack' of something, but finally, ultimately it comes out of fullness, love and joy.

'It is meet and right' expresses all this. It is the only possible response to the divine invitation to live and to receive abundant life.[3]

This is not to say that *the* Eucharist – the Mass or Holy Communion or whatever you call it – is the most important thing in life. But that service does stand for and symbolize something that really is at the core of Christian existence: thanksgiving. In giving thanks we return God's works to him in gratitude and receive the world back from his hands with joy and trust. This is part of the Christian definition of what it is to be truly human. Thanksgiving is the chief purpose for which human beings were made: to give God thanks and praise. This is not to imply that God wants plenty of admirers to sing his praises, at whatever cost to themselves! Rather, God makes thanksgiving not only a duty but also a joy. When we enjoy music or gardening or driving or making love, we are taken out of ourselves, and we automatically feel thankful; and giving thanks is all we need to do. People who have never learned to feel thankful live impover-ished lives in which they are never taken out of themselves; they are missing out on one of the great things about being human.

Christians in their ministry to others have the duty, which is also a pleasure, to help them to identify causes for thankfulness, and to assist them in giving thanks. Of course they also have the obligation of standing alongside others in grief and tragedy. If I have said little about that, it is because it is more obvious to many people than is this role in times of thanksgiving. Ministry tends readily to be seen in terms of helping the afflicted. While it does certainly involve that, it is important not to ignore its positive task of helping people to rejoice. Christians involved in ministry are committed to becoming the kind of people to whom giving thanks comes naturally, who can recognize the good hand of God in some of the events that happen in the world, and who want to give thanks for this themselves and to help others to do so, too.

Eucharist, giving thanks, is the primary task of the ordained Christian, and it may be called a priestly task. If so, then there are many lay people in the churches who are also in that sense priests – while there are some who are ordained who do not display any authentically priestly traits, since they have not learned to give thanks, to be taken out of themselves in order to give praise and glory to God. What such people have never acquired is the ability to be spontaneous in thankfulness. But there are many Christians around who can teach them, people who light up the lives of others and enable them to flourish. One cannot help in making people flourish without having in one's own heart the kind of gladness I have been trying to describe, which requires the peculiar combination of empathy and detachment this chapter and the preceding one are intended to illustrate.

1 For an English translation see Thomas Mann, *Death in Venice; Tristan; Tonio Kröger* (trans. by H. T. Lowe-Porter, Harmondsworth: Penguin, 1986). The passage quoted on pp. 65–6 is my own translation from the German.

2 Gregory Dix, *The Shape of the Liturgy* (London: Dacre Press and Adam & Charles Black, 1945), p. xviii.
3 Alexander Schmemann, *The World as Sacrament* (London: Darton, Longman & Todd, 1966), pp. 44–5.

7. Surprised by Joy

'Rejoice in the Lord always; again I will say, Rejoice' (Philippians 4.4). 'Always' is a long time, and St Paul's words need to be an imperative, because so often the call to be joyful goes against our natural instincts. Much of the time there seems little to be joyful about in life, and rejoicing all the time seems as unnatural as does giving thanks all the time. Our instinct is, as Ecclesiastes might have put it, that there is a time to be joyful and a time to refrain from rejoicing. There is something unnatural about people who are always cheerful, come what may. Most of us, for example, have attended funerals at which we were exhorted not to feel any grief but to rejoice in the hope of the resurrection, and have felt that this is rather too good to be true: there is a time to grieve, and though rejoicing may come, now is not yet the time for it. I remember once being particularly offended by the artificial cheerfulness of a funeral for a baby who had died by cot-death – surely not the kind of occasion on which to tell the mourners to 'rejoice always'. Joy cannot and should not be manufactured in this way; if it comes to desolate people, it comes unbidden.

That in fact is the first thing to be said about joy. It is a grace, a surprise, something that bursts on us when we are not expecting it, as Wordsworth captured in his line 'surprised by joy' (which C. S. Lewis famously borrowed as the title of his autobiography).[1] There *is* such a thing as a steady and settled joy, as we shall see later, but it is not a thing of fixed and forced grins, and to understand joy it is important to start with the kind that comes unbidden. Surprising joy arises primarily out of a reversal of fortune, when things that were wrong suddenly come right, and the world that appeared grey and dull is illuminated and multi-coloured again.

J. R. R. Tolkien has a memorable discussion of Christian joy and its relation to a sudden happy outcome in his lecture 'On Fairy Stories', written in 1947. He speaks of

> The Consolation of the Happy Ending. Almost I would venture to say that all complete fairy-stories must have it. At least I would say that Tragedy is the true form of Drama, its highest function; but the opposite is true of Fairy-story. Since we do not appear to possess a word that expresses this opposite – I will call it *Eucatastrophe*. The *eucatastrophic* tale is the true form of fairy-tale, and its highest function.

> The consolation of fairy-stories, the joy of the happy ending or more correctly of the good catastrophe, the sudden joyous 'turn': this joy, which is one of the things which fairy-stories can produce supremely well, is not essentially 'escapist', nor 'fugitive'. In its fairytale – or

otherworld – setting, it is a sudden and miraculous grace; never to be counted on to recur. It does not deny the existence of … sorrow and failure …; it denies (in the face of much evidence, if you will) universal final defeat and in so far is *evangelium*, giving a fleeting glimpse of Joy, Joy beyond the walls of the world, poignant as grief.

In such stories when the 'turn' comes we get a piercing … joy, and heart's desire, that for a moment passes outside the frame, rends indeed the very web of story, and lets a gleam come through.[2]

Tolkien talks of the *eucatastrophe* as what unites fairytale with the Christian drama, the 'happy ending' but in a much more profound sense than in an ordinary comedy. This ending creates a feeling that not only the plot of the story but in some way the whole world has been restored, renewed, resurrected. As essential feature of the eucatastrophic reversal is a radical discontinuity between old and new, before and after.

For Christians the archetypal moment of joy comes with the resurrection of Christ, bringing light and gladness out of utter misery and darkness. The creeds do not adequately capture this – they are not the sort of document that could. They seem to present the events of salvation in a very two-dimensional way, like a checklist: Christ was born of the Virgin Mary, suffered under Pontius Pilate, was crucified, died, was buried, rose again on the third day, ascended into heaven, sits at the right hand of the Father. It is all very deadpan. To catch a sense of the earth-shattering truth behind this dull catalogue we need

Bach's B-minor Mass. Modern music centres can rise to the challenge, but on my old record-player you could not hear the 'Crucifixus' unless you had the volume so high that the 'Et resurrexit' deafened you and made it sound as though the room was about to explode. If you had a reasonable volume for the 'Et resurrexit' you lost the 'Crucifixus' altogether. This, though irritating, strikes me as very right and proper. The crucifixion and the resurrection belong in different orders of reality; they are not just successive events on a single time-line. The string of events recorded in the creed has an infinitely deep rift in it, the space between death and new life.

For me, the meaning of Christ's resurrection is captured perfectly in John 20, where the terror and agony of the Passion are replaced, not by a matching act of power and vengeance, but by a man and a woman meeting in the cool of the morning in a garden and recognizing each other, their pain now irreversibly past. 'Jesus said to her, "Mary." She said to him, "Rabboni."' This sense comes across in a mediaeval poem translated by Helen Waddell:

Last night did Christ the Sun rise from the dark,
    The mystic harvest of the fields of God,
And now the little wandering tribes of bees
    Are brawling in the scarlet flowers abroad.
The winds are soft with birdsong; all night long
    Darkling the nightingale her descant told,
And now inside church doors the happy folk
    The Alleluia chant a hundredfold.
O father of thy folk, be thine by right
The Easter joy, the threshold of the light.[3]

If there is to be joy in our own lives, it will have to share something of this quality: complete reversal, followed by calm and delight.

Over thirty years ago Harry Williams described how language about resurrection can resonate with the experiences of ordinary life in his book *True Resurrection*. This offended some by a rather reductionist tone, as though the story of Jesus' resurrection were no more than a kind of model or template that helped us to recognize 'real' resurrections when they occurred in our own lives. But there is no reason why someone who believes very firmly in the reality of Christ's literal resurrection should not find that it both illuminates and is illuminated by other events, large and small, that show a similar pattern of sudden reversal. Williams shows how resurrection can become real in our daily lives in a passage where he talks about ethics:

Living goodness ... must be the result of renewed creativity, and it will manifest itself not in terms of realizing values which exist already in some changeless ideal realm above and beyond man, but in terms of actually creating values which are new. 'The task of ethics is not to draw up a list of traditional moral norms, but to have the daring to make creative valuations.' And values can thus be created only by being lived, not by being argued about ... This creation of new values means that for us to enter eternity and be given eternal life is not to be raised up to the vision of some static state of changeless perfection, but to participate more and more actively in the creative processes we find all around us here and now. To be raised from the dead by the creative call of the Eternal Word is to find that we are ourselves agents of resurrection. And to be ourselves agents of resurrection, raising men from enslavement to their own dead past, is the true meaning of ethical behaviour. Goodness, in other words, is the expression of superabundant life. It is our way of endlessly becoming more and more of what we are, so that other people are enabled to do so also. It is the overflowing of joy – the joy which brings life to everybody it meets.[4]

The joy of the resurrection of Christ, which can seem so abstract a concept to many people, takes shape in our lives in a transformation of the way we live. As the epistle to the Colossians puts it, 'If you have been raised with Christ, seek the things that are above, where Christ is, seated at the right hand of God' (3.1). The life of someone who has experienced the joy that comes from resurrection will never be the same again: it will have a sort of exuberant creativity, making other people flourish by the way it is lived.

One place where the kind of reversal expressed in resurrection can be seen is in recovery from illness, particularly where this is unexpected. We might revisit our friends Bob and Wendy from Chapter 2. Both of them have experienced the way pain can remit. For Bob, remission is usually gradual, and there is a continuum between sickness and health that perhaps seldom produces the elation and joy of reversal – just as, on the other hand, he seldom suffers real despair, because his illness impedes but does not completely threaten his normal life. Wendy, however, represents reversal in a classic form. Her depression sometimes remits with great suddenness, startling for other people but in a way even more startling for her. It feels as unexpected as a sudden thaw after days of frost and ice, or a crocus suddenly one morning appearing in the snow. And it results in a great period of contentment and peace, before a return to the ordinary routine of life makes the delight fade into something more mundane, though still very pleasant. A near analogy for most of us might be the feeling you get when you've had a feverish illness – flu, bronchitis – and your temperature goes down to normal; your chest stops constricting and constraining you, and you can go out for a short walk and then rest and relax, knowing that you'll soon be quite better. Whether on a large or small scale, whether after physical illness or mental horror, the experience is a resurrection, the triumph of light over darkness. Surprising joy is like this: not a steady state, not something on which we can insist by trying to master our natural feelings, but a relaxed sense of delight that steals up on us and transforms our experience without our needing, or being able, to do anything about it.

Joy is a gift. It is what would once have been called, in theological jargon, an infused virtue, something we receive, rather than a task at which we work. The joy of the resurrection in the New Testament is, precisely, joy that something unexpected has happened, to which no human being has made the least contribution: it is gratuitous. And the effect of such joy is that it temporarily removes from us all sense that there is anything in particular that we ought to be doing. When we recover from the flu, there are a few days when all we can do is to potter around rather gently, and when that is also all we ought to be doing. Convalescence is very closely related to joy, and its weakness can be a positive pleasure, hinting at the eternal Sabbaths for which we are supposed to be preparing: it's strange how Christians who pray that the departed may enjoy eternal rest are often so far from knowing how to enjoy the temporal kind.

Because joy thus comes unbidden and as a gift, we cannot say that Christians have a duty to be joyful in quite the same way as they have a duty to be thankful: thanksgiving is an activity you do, joy is something that happens to you. It is, as Walt Whitman put it, 'as the sun falling around a helpless thing'.[5] We can recognize it, but we cannot coerce it. Our willingness to let other people share in our joy is to some extent a test of how far we have really recognized the experience, and evangelism makes sense only if that is what it amounts to – sharing our joy with others, not trying to force ideas down their throats. The parable of the woman who lost the coin, and when she found it called her neighbours together to share in her rejoicing, is presented in the Gospels as a model for the joy in heaven over one sinner who repents, and no doubt that is so. But it only works as an illustration for someone who understands the kind of human joy that the parable presupposes, and who has experience of rejoicing with others in their good luck. If you cannot do that, then you do not understand what joy is anyway, and you certainly cannot share the good news of the gospel. We are all merely recipients of the joy God gives, and in this we are all equal. As the Oxford Tube (an Oxford-London bus service) used to say in its advertisements: 'Every ticket economy, every seat first-class.'

1 C. S. Lewis, *Surprised by Joy: The Shape of my Early Life* (London: Geoffrey Bles, 1955); the most recent edition is in *C. S. Lewis Signature Classics* (London: HarperCollins, 2002), vol. 7. Wordsworth's sonnet 'Surprised by Joy' is in fact among his most mournful!

2 J. R. R. Tolkien, 'On Fairy-stories', in *Essays Presented to Charles Williams* (London: Oxford University Press, 1947); reprinted with minor revisions in *Tree and Leaf* (London: Unwin, 1964), pp. 11–70.

3 Sedulius Scottus (*fl.* 848–74), 'Carmen Paschale', translated in Helen Waddell, *Medieval Latin Lyrics* (London: Constable, 1929; Penguin, 1952), pp. 130–1.

4 H. A. Williams, *True Resurrection* (London: Mitchell Beazley, 1972), p. 116. The internal quotation is from N. Berdyaev, *The Destiny of Man* (London: Geoffrey Bles, 1937), p. 20.

5 Walt Whitman, 'By Blue Ontario's Shores'.

8. Always Rejoicing

St Paul's injunction to 'rejoice in the Lord always' has so far seemed to present something of a problem. Joy is something we cannot control; it comes unsought. The event in Christian memory and belief it corresponds to, the resurrection of Christ, is itself an unexpected and unlooked-for event, which breaks into all our natural emotions and responses, not a steady or settled state of affairs. It is possible to say that Christians should always be joyful because, since the first Easter, Christ is always risen, so there is never again any reason for gloom or despondency. But most people's psychology cannot really operate on so high a level. Our life has alternations of light and shade, happiness and unhappiness, and genuinely continual joy is not a real option for most people. What passes for it, a kind of terrible fixed grin or immoveable heartiness of manner, is so obviously not the genuine article.

There is a kind of 'steady state' joy, however, which we need to approach in a rather different way. In Chapter 4 we looked at the question of 'the meaning of life'; and I suggested that an interest in this can be one of two things.

It can be a quest for *the* meaning of life: the one thing that makes it all hang together. Following Freud, I urged that this interest is often a sign of mental illness. Like most theologians, I frequently receive letters from people who have discovered the meaning of life in this sense. They are written in green or purple ink on lined paper, and they usually warn me that the world's failure to perceive the meaning of life is about to lead to an apocalyptic end to the universe. But the second thing we might be interested in is what we might call the meaningfulness of life, the fact that it is not empty or chaotic or meaning*less*. Where the search for 'the meaning of life' can lead into (or arise from) strange psychological distortions, perceiving the world as meaningful is by contrast a benign and mature state of mind – the normal state of mind of most people in most ages and most cultures. They do not ask why they should bother to work, or to marry, or to bring up children, why they should live at peace with their neighbours. They do not constantly say, 'What's the point of it all?' Living life is its own justification.

Now out of this healthy and balanced attitude to the life we are given to live in the world, there can arise what I would call a 'steady state' joy that has less to do with sudden disclosures of the kind we looked at in the previous chapter, and more to do with an ongoing sense of appropriateness or fittingness in things. To see the world, despite all its terrible evils, as nevertheless worth living in, produces something we could also call joy, even though it lacks the surprise and wonder we have considered so far.

Joy in this sense is a feeling of thankfulness and delight that there is a world, and that it is possible to do worthwhile things in it. It is not justified only when we have somehow identified our destiny and are fulfilling it, so that otherwise the world is a blank and meaningless place. It is valid simply as the recognition that God made all things, and behold, they were very good. This is a natural state of the healthy mind, and is not related to what we or anyone else have or have not achieved. It is perfectly compatible with pleasure in achievement; but achievement is superimposed on a basic sense of affirmation and acceptance of the world, rather than as the only thing that makes our life worthwhile – which is a considerably less healthy state to be in. Life is affirmed as worthwhile in itself. Human activity, including Wendy's knitting, does not need elaborate justification.

Sometimes joy that things are so, that the world is as it is, can tip over into a kind of ecstasy just as exciting as the joy of reversal. Browning wrote, 'God's in his heaven, all's right with the world' in response to the fact that 'the lark's on the wing, the snail's on the thorn'.[1] It is very easy to deride this as fatuous optimism when set alongside all the ills of the world, and to talk as though Browning was simply shutting his eyes to them. Nature looks wonderful, but the lark on the wing is probably preparing to eat the snail on the thorn. But in itself Browning's lines are simply a rather extreme expression of a delight that does not have to be justified by specifying what, then, precisely, is 'right with the world'. Well before Browning we find an expression of this kind of near-ecstasy at the mere fact that things are as they are in Thomas Traherne's *Centuries of Meditation*, written in about 1672:

Your enjoyment of the world is never right, till you so esteem it, that everything in it, is more your treasure than a King's exchequer full of Gold and Silver ... Can you take too much joy in your Father's works? He is Himself in everything.[2]

[When I was a child] the corn was orient and immortal wheat, which never should be reaped, nor was ever sown. I thought it had stood from everlasting to everlasting. The dust and stones of the street were as precious as gold ... The green trees when I saw them first through one of the gates transported and ravished me, their sweetness and unusual beauty made my heart to leap ... Eternity was manifest in the light of the day, and something infinite behind everything appeared.[3]

Well, maybe this is slightly over the top, and a psychiatrist might suspect something a bit manic – though so far as we know Traherne was a perfectly balanced person. What he is expressing, in these exaggerated terms, is the sense that created things, rightly considered, bear witness to the glory of their creator. A Christian might say that he is not finding too much meaning in things, but rather is one of the few writers who really does understand what God meant by saying that what he had made was 'very good'.

A strange but rather important aspect of this kind of joy, the joy that things just are as they are, is the creation of lists. Taxonomists of all sorts, from librarians to botanists, know the satisfaction of finding an orderly way of grasping reality. (The passage from Traherne, indeed, is in full a list of the things that he marvelled at.) This psychology of listing as a way of celebrating the world lies very deep in human consciousness. Lists are often not utilitarian, but celebratory. The essence of listing can be seen in a poem by P. J. Kavanagh:

A year ago I fell in love with the functional ward
Of a chest hospital; square cubicles in a row,
Plain concrete, wash basins – an art lover's woe,
Not counting how the fellow in the next bed snored.
But nothing whatever is by love debarred
The common and banal her heart can know.
The corridor led to a stairway and below
Was the inexhaustible adventure of a gravelled yard.
This is what love does to things: the Rialto Bridge,
The main gate that was bent by a heavy lorry,
The seat at the back of a shed that was a suntrap.
Naming these things is the love-act and its pledges:
For we must record love's mystery without claptrap.
Snatch out of time the passionate transitory.[4]

George Herbert (1593–1633) had a vivid image for the list-making mentality:

Of all the creatures both in sea and land
Onely to man thou hast made known thy wayes
And put the penne alone into his hand
And made him Secretarie of thy praise.[5]

And he himself provides one of the finest examples of it in his sonnet 'Prayer':

Prayer the Churches banquet, Angels age,
    Gods breath in man returning to his birth,
    The soul in paraphrase, heart in pilgrimage,
The Christian plummet sounding heav'n and earth;
Engine against th' Almightie, sinners towre,
    Reversed thunder, Christ-side-piercing spear,
    The six-daies world transposing in an hour,
A kind of tune, which all things heare and fear;
Softnesse, and peace, and joy, and love, and blisse,
    Exalted Manna, gladnesse of the best,
    Heaven in ordinarie, man well drest,
The milkie way, the bird of Paradise,
    Church-bels beyond the starres heard, the souls bloud,
    The land of spices; something understood.[6]

Listing is an extraordinarily life-affirming activity. Here is an affectionate example from Alan Bennett's collection *Writing Home*, which lives in the world he has made his own through the TV series 'Talking Heads', the rather gritty, ordinary world of front rooms, dentures, seaside promenades, and rent-books (there's another list). There is a humour but also a kindness and human care about it:

My mother's description of her clothes:
    My other shoes
    My warm boots
    My tweedy coat
    The greeny coat of mine
    That fuzzy blue coat I have
    My coat with the round buttons[7]

– 'like the inventory of a medieval will', he comments.

Besides cataloguing joy, listing can also assist in sorrow, as can be seen from the custom of reading the list of those killed in action, on Remembrance Sunday. Speaking the names is a powerful act which reaffirms these people and re-establishes them again as part of our world, not forgotten but still present. Lists can of course also be ludicrous. Some readers may be familiar with the journalist Beachcomber's 'Anthology of Huntingdonshire Cabmen', a simple listing of the most ridiculous real and made-up names, solemnly read out each week on television thirty years ago by Sir Michael Redgrave in a programme loosely co-ordinated by Spike Milligan. But, in serious uses, listing orders the world yet without changing it, and that is an important component of the kind of joy we are concerned with at the moment. Listing does not *impart* meaning to things, still less *the* meaning; it affirms that things are already meaningful.

Such joy implies that things are appropriate, that the steady state of the world, even without great deeds being done to change it, is not empty, but full of significance and utterly worthwhile. But an authentic Christian version of this perhaps requires a combination of the two sorts of joy we have been looking at, for steady state joy alone is not enough. The world may indeed be good and worthwhile, but it is nevertheless a place in which hideous evils occur. According to the gospel God does not only look at this world and declare that it is very good, but also enters into it to renew and reform it when it goes wrong. Too much emphasis on rejoicing in the steady state can produce complacency, a refusal to confront the evil in the world.

On the other hand, too much emphasis on the joy of reversal, on salvation and redemption, can leave the world into which we return after evil has been reversed curiously empty of meaning. When people have been through a terrible and traumatic experience they need the assurance that the world is not constituted simply of that experience and its reversal, but has been ticking over in a satisfactory way while it was waiting for them to return. Where that sense is absent, they can become detached from the ordinary world and unable to enter it again. One sees this in the experiences of some survivors of the Nazi camps, who were able to rejoice in their own liberation but for whom the world had been so marred by the blot put on it through Nazism and its consequences that they could never enjoy even simple, ordinary pleasures again. Many Holocaust survivors committed suicide. People say that this is because they bore a weight of guilt for having survived when so many others died, and for all I know this may be so. But I wonder whether in some cases it may have been the experience which afflicts many who have endured horrific suffering, that they can no longer see the world as sound and healthy: re-entry is impossible because there is no good world to re-enter. As Paul Celan put it in a poem, one can be walking along a quiet road at evening, when suddenly 'the scar of time', which has never properly healed, is ripped open, and snarling dogs pour out to lay waste the landscape, killing as they go[8] – like the dogs in the death camps. Joy is no longer a possibility for a person with such an experience; they are, in effect, in a permanent depression. When they commit suicide, their death is as much the work of their original jailers as if they had executed them.

But for those of us who have known fewer extremes of suffering, a steady state joy is possible, and needs to exist alongside the joy that surprises us, and comes from reversal. We need Genesis as well as the Resurrection Narratives. We need to rejoice in the world, in our daily lives, in the unspectacular satisfactoriness of just being; just as we need also the experience of seeing our world turned from darkness to light, from silence to singing.

1 *Pippa Passes* (1841).
2 Thomas Traherne, *Centuries* I.28 (London: The Faith Press, 1960), p. 14.
3 *Centuries* III.3, p. 110.
4 P. J. Kavanagh, 'The Hospital', *Collected Poems* (London, 1972); quoted in D. W. Hardy and D. F. Ford, *Jubilate: Theology in Praise* (London: Darton, Longman & Todd, 1984), p. 71. Hardy's and Ford's book is an extended discussion of the possibility of basing a whole theology on the idea of praise, and I am very much indebted to it.
5 George Herbert, 'Providence', *The Poems of George Herbert* (London: Oxford University Press, 1971), p. 107.
6 'Prayer (1)', *The Poems of George Herbert*, p. 44.
7 Alan Bennett, *Writing Home* (London: Faber and Faber, 1994), p. 280.
8 Paul Celan, 'Abend der Worte', *Die Hand voller Stunden und andere Gedichte* (Munich: Deutscher Taschenbuch Verlag, 1991), p. 77.